公共英语
版系列教材

新发展高职英语
综合教程 ①

New
Development

College English
Comprehensive Course

总 主 编　王永祥
主　　编　章国军　舒立志

副主编　欧　洁　钟丽君
编　者　黄淑玲　李　华　蒋　琳
　　　　吴艳华　周　洁

北京理工大学出版社
BEIJING INSTITUTE OF TECHNOLOGY PRESS

版权专有　侵权必究

图书在版编目（CIP）数据

新发展高职英语综合教程.1/章国军，舒立志主编.--北京：北京理工大学出版社，2021.8（2022.9重印）
高职高专公共英语智慧云版系列教材/王永祥主编
ISBN 978-7-5763-0162-5

Ⅰ.①新… Ⅱ.①章…②舒… Ⅲ.①英语—高等职业教育—教材 Ⅳ.①H319.39

中国版本图书馆CIP数据核字(2021)第161149号

出版发行 /	北京理工大学出版社有限责任公司
社　　址 /	北京市海淀区中关村南大街5号
邮　　编 /	100081
电　　话 /	（010）68914775（总编室）
	（010）82562903（教材售后服务热线）
	（010）68944723（其他图书服务热线）
网　　址 /	http://www.bitpress.com.cn
经　　销 /	全国各地新华书店
印　　刷 /	沂南县汶凤印刷有限公司
开　　本 /	889毫米×1194毫米　1/16
印　　张 /	12.5
字　　数 /	245千字
版　　次 /	2021年8月第1版　2022年9月第2次印刷
定　　价 /	49.80元
责任编辑 /	武丽娟
文案编辑 /	武丽娟
责任校对 /	刘亚男
责任印制 /	施胜娟

图书出现印装质量问题，请拨打售后服务热线，本社负责调换

FOREWORD

系统功能语言学创始人韩礼德（M. A. K. Halliday）在其"以语言为基础的学习理论"（Towards a Language-based Theory of Learning, 1993）一文中指出，语言学习包含三个方面：学习语言（learning language）、通过语言学习（learning through language）、学习语言知识（learning about language）。学习语言知识很容易做到，绝大多数外语教材和外语课堂均能实现。而广大外语教育工作者并不满足于此，他们懂得，外语学习的目的不仅仅是获得各种语言知识，还需要掌握各种语言技能，需要能够真正听懂外语、讲好外语、读懂外语、写好外语，即真正地"学习语言"，从而培养交际能力。除了"学习语言"和"学习语言知识"以外，语言学习还有一个非常重要的目的，那就是"通过语言学习"。对学习者而言，所谓"通过语言学习"就是运用语言学习各种不同领域的专业知识和技能。因此，高职英语教学必然包含一项重要任务——帮助学生运用英语学习各种职场知识。

为全面贯彻《高等职业教育专科英语课程标准》（2021版）和《高职高专教育英语课程教学基本要求》的精神，并基于上文所述理念，编者编写了《新发展高职英语综合教程》系列教材。本套教材涵盖高等职业教育专科阶段英语学科必须具备的四大核心素养：职场涉外沟通、多元文化交流、语言思维提升和自主学习完善。通过本套教材的学习，学生能够达到课程标准所设定的四项学科核心素养的发展目标，即职场涉外沟通目标、多元文化交流目标、语言思维提升目标和自主学习完善目标。

本套教材共3册。第1册将高职学生在校三年主要的典型环节缩影于第一学期，让学生在开学之初适应中职或者高中阶段与高职阶段学习的同时，对未来高职三年的整体学习获得宏观了解，并树立职业目标，做好职业规划。第2册则聚焦各行各业中的共核技能并进行提炼和整合，侧重具体的职业知识和职业技能，重点培养学生的专业知识和职业能力。第3册主要突出职业提升，在职业提升中兼顾素养提升和学业提升。

本套教材内容丰富，包括职业与个人、职业与社会、职业与环境三大主题。每册每个单元围绕具体主题进行不同模块的设计，包括热身练习（Warm-up）、主课文（Reading A）、听说（Listening and speaking）、副课文（Reading B）、应用写作（Applied writing）、项目操练（Project performing）、语法（Grammar）、自我评价（Self-evaluation）、文化（Culture）等。这些模块既有语言知识（语法）和语言技能（听说读写）的训练，也有语言在职场中的具体运用。

《新发展高职英语综合教程》践行以运用为导向的高职英语教学理念，助力广大高职院校英语教师实现高职英语教学中语言知识、语言能力与语言运用的融合，实现对韩礼德所阐述的语言学习三个方面（"学习语言""通过语言学习"和"学习语言知识"）的全覆盖。

王永祥

2021年夏于南京仙林湖畔

  《新发展高职英语综合教程 1》由北京理工大学出版社开发，国内数名英语教育专家共同设计，国家示范性高职院校建设单位、国家优质高职院校、国家"双高计划"建设单位广东轻工职业技术学院多名具有丰富教学经验和一线企业实践经验的骨干教师参与编写，是一本兼具国际化、网络化、立体化、人文化的高职英语教材。

  一、编写依据

  《新发展高职英语综合教程 1》全面贯彻《高等职业教育专科英语课程标准》（2021版）的精神，在设计与编写中融入关于"课程目标"和"课程内容"的最新要求，内容涵盖职业与个人、职业与社会、职业与环境三大主题，并在细分专题中重点纳入职业规划、社会责任等话题。与此同时，本教材借鉴近年来高职英语教学领域的成功经验与教学成果，吸取国内外先进的外语教学理念与教学方法，以高职院校人才培养主要环节为依据选取教学内容，层次分明、结构紧凑、特点突出。

  本教材以高职院校学生为教学对象，针对此类院校的生源特点、培养目标和教学特色，使课堂学习与自主学习相结合、线上与线下学习相结合，满足混合式教学需求；在此基础上，充分挖掘合适的多媒体素材，丰富课堂教学内容。

  二、教材特色

  作为高职人才培养的基地和主体，高职院校堪称高职人才步入职场、融入社会之前逐步提升自身能力、完善自身素养的"孵化室"。高职院校人才培养过程是其人才方案的具体体现，关乎高职人才培养的质量和人才产出的规格，理应为高职院校师生和用人单位所熟悉，以便高职教师能据此确定教学内容、设计教学模式，高职学生能据此设定学习目标、规划职业生涯，用人单位能据此介入人才培养、推进产教融合。当下流行的各种高职外语类教材要么仅对高职校园生活稍稍触及，要么仅对职场文化大书特书，罕有对人才培养过程的深入探讨。本教材基于高职人才培养的主要环节设计教学内容，力图填补这一空白。

本教材在广泛调研的基础上，根据目前我国高职高专大学生的实际英语水平与英语学习条件，力图突破传统教学模式的局限性，在教学理念、教学内容、教学方法等方面坚持创新，充分体现以学习者为中心，融"教、学、练"为一体的教学理念。

1. 注重综合文化素养的培育，素质与能力双培养

以学生为主体、教师为主导。本教材在选材与练习活动设计中均融入课程思政元素，综合世界各国的文化知识和中国传统价值观念，注重思政教育、德育教育和人文熏陶，使学生既具有国际视野，又能够运用英语讲述中国故事，进而培养学生的综合文化素养。

2. 夯实英语语言基础，激发学习兴趣，培养思辨能力

真实的语境、生动的语料、灵活的练习。本教材致力于提高学生在不同情境下的语言应用能力，帮助学生夯实语言基础，综合培养学生的听、说、读、写、译等语言技能，并通过启发性、思辨性的练习设计，启迪学生思考，提高思辨能力。

3. 选材具有鲜明的中国特色，兼具中国情怀与国际视野

本教材在内容选择上重点关注中国情怀和国际视野，兼具职业与个人、职业与社会、职业与环境三大主题，贴近高职学校人才培养全过程，侧重选取能反映社会与产业界对高职人才能力和素质综合要求的教学素材，具有育人性、实用性、职业性、时效性等特点，力图为综合型高技能实用人才的培养增值赋能。

4. 丰富的视频资源，提供鲜活、地道的语言使用情境和练习

本教材每个单元均提供了与主题相关的大量视频，以便深化学生对单元主题的理解，强化学生对英语语言知识和语言技能的掌握，拓展学生的语言学习体验。

三、单元模块设计

本教材每个单元分为单元目标（Learning objectives）、热身练习（Warm-up）、主课文（Reading A）、听说（Listening and speaking）、副课文（Reading B）、应用写作（Applied writing）、项目操练（Project performing）、语法（Grammar）、自我评价（Self-evaluation）、文化（Culture）十个教学环节，具体使用说明如下：

1. 单元目标（Learning objectives）

该部分为每单元的整体教学目标，旨在说明学生完成本单元的学习后应该掌握的各类知识以及英语综合语言应用能力。

2. 热身练习（Warm-up）

该部分为每单元的第一学习阶段，旨在通过形式多样的练习任务引导学生就单元主题进行口头表达，以便为主课文的学习做好准备。

3. 主课文（Reading A）

该部分为每单元的第二学习阶段，旨在通过对主课文的阅读使学生对单元主题有宏观的了解，并借助阅读前、阅读后的各种练习任务加深对主课文的理解。与单元主题的关系相比，主课文的内容相对较为宽泛。

4. 听说（Listening and speaking）

该部分为每单元的第三学习阶段，旨在通过与单元主题相关的4个情景对话或独白加深学生对单元主题的认识。本部分设计了两项与单元主题相关的口语表达任务，以便学生进行口头输出训练，培养英语口语表达能力。

5. 副课文（Reading B）

该部分为每单元的第四学习阶段，旨在通过对副课文的阅读进一步强化学生对单元主题的了解，并借助读后练习任务加深学生对副课文的理解。与单元主题的关系相比，副课文的内容相对较为具体。

6. 应用写作（Applied writing）

该部分为每单元的第五学习阶段，旨在通过与单元主题相关的应用文写作任务对学生进行书面输出训练，培养英语应用写作能力。

7. 项目操练（Project performing）

该部分为每单元的第六学习阶段，旨在通过集小组讨论、角色扮演、口头陈述于一体的综合性项目巩固学生对单元主题的全面把握。

8. 语法（Grammar）

该部分为每单元的第七学习阶段，旨在通过一些特殊用法讲解及相应的练习任务对学生的语法知识进行查漏补缺，以提升其语言输出的准确性。

9. 自我评价（Self-evaluation）

该部分为每单元的第八学习阶段，旨在通过自我评价表使学生对自己是否达到单元目标中的知识或能力要求做出客观评价。

10. 文化（Culture）

该部分为每单元的第九学习阶段，旨在通过富含中国元素、中国精神的视频短片从中国人的视角对学生进行课程思政教育，增强其对中华文化的自信心和自豪感。

此外，为进一步凸显六个单元主题之间的内在逻辑联系，本教材以虚构的高职院校学生李明（Li Ming）为主角贯穿全书，按照人才培养主要环节的基本流程将每个单元的教学内容设计为一幕幕的"剧情"，展现李明在学校语境中由高职学生逐步向未来职场人演进的整个"剧本"，反映了学校、职场、社会在合力打造职场新人过程中发挥的不同作用。

本教材由王永祥教授担任总主编，负责教材的总框架设计、选文审核及定稿审核等工作。章国军教授和舒立志副教授担任主编，分别负责单元主题及体例确定、各单元编写材料的审定与统稿以及各单元编写任务的分配与落实、各单元统稿与初审的工作。舒立志副教授还负责阅读文章A篇的编写。欧洁和钟丽君老师担任副主编，分别负责语法模块、应用文写作及项目活动模块模块。黄淑玲老师负责练习部分的编写。李华老师负责阅读文章B篇的编写。蒋琳老师负责热身模块的编写。吴艳华老师负责听说模块的编写。周洁老师负责文化模块的编写。

由于编者水平有限，本教材在编写过程中难免存在纰漏之处，敬请各位读者及相关院校师生在使用过程中批评指正，以便编者能够及时修订并加以完善，更好地服务于高职人才培养。

编　者

2021年8月

CONTENTS

Unit 1
College Major Choices

- Warm-up ··· 2
- Reading A ··· 3
- Listening and speaking ··· 8
- Reading B ··· 11
- Applied writing ··· 18
- Project performing ··· 20
- Grammar ··· 21
- Self-evaluation ··· 24
- Culture ··· 25

Unit 2
Autonomous Learning

- Warm-up ··· 28
- Reading A ··· 30
- Listening and speaking ··· 35
- Reading B ··· 38
- Applied writing ··· 45
- Project performing ··· 47
- Grammar ··· 48
- Self-evaluation ··· 51
- Culture ··· 52

Unit 3
On-campus Training

Warm-up	56
Reading A	58
Listening and speaking	62
Reading B	65
Applied writing	72
Project performing	74
Grammar	75
Self-evaluation	78
Culture	79

Unit 4
Community Service

Warm-up	82
Reading A	83
Listening and speaking	88
Reading B	91
Applied writing	99
Project performing	101
Grammar	102
Self-evaluation	105
Culture	106

Unit 5
Post Internships

Warm-up	108
Reading A	109
Listening and speaking	113
Reading B	116
Applied writing	124
Project performing	126
Grammar	127
Self-evaluation	130
Culture	131

Unit 6
Campus Recruitment

- Warm-up 134
- Reading A 136
- Listening and speaking 141
- Reading B 144
- Applied writing 151
- Project performing 153
- Grammar 154
- Self-evaluation 157
- Culture 158

Word List

- New words & expressions 160
- Glossary 172
- Proper names 188

Unit 1
College Major Choices

Learning objectives

After studying this unit, you should be able to:
- get familiar with the words and expressions concerning college majors and major choices;
- have some idea of what factors you have to take into consideration when choosing a college major;
- know whom you may consult with when choosing a college major;
- be clear what majors are the best ones for the future;
- master the skills of writing a notice;
- be expert at the special usages of nouns.

Warm-up

Task 1 Watch the video and role-play the dialogue with your partner. One of the good ways to do this is to copy down the subtitles first, and then practice them orally. Some key words and phrases are listed for you.

freshman 大一新生	exchange program 交换生项目	sophomore 大二学生
workload 工作量	major 主修	minor 辅修

Task 2 Work with your partner. Try to give the Chinese meanings of the following 6 college majors with the help of a dictionary. Then match each of them with the corresponding pictures.

A. Electrical Engineering
B. Nursing
C. Physical Therapy
D. Pharmacology
E. Construction Management
F. Aeronautics and Aviation Technology

1 (　)

2 (　)

3 (　)

4 (　)

5 (　)

6 (　)

Reading A

Li Ming, a freshman just in college, is facing the problem of choosing a right major, but he doesn't know what major he should choose. Can you give him any advice on how to choose a major?

Pre-reading questions

1. What is a college major?
2. What were the important factors that influenced your major choice?

How to choose a major

With the high cost of college tuition, it is imperative to choose your major wisely. Consider the following factors when picking your major.

1. Career prep

Choose a major because it will prepare you for a specific career path or advanced study. Maybe you already know that you want to be a nurse, a day trader, a physical therapist, or a web developer. Before you declare, take a class or two in the relevant discipline, check out the syllabus for an advanced seminar, and talk to students in the department of your choice. Make sure you're ready for the coursework required for the career of your dreams.

2. Earning potential

Future earning potential is worth considering. College is a big investment, and while college can pay you back in many ways beyond salary, this can be a major factor for students who are paying their own way or taking out loans. According to PayScale.com, the majors that lead to the highest salaries include just about any type of engineering, actuarial mathematics, computer science, physics, statistics, and economics. Keep your quality of life in mind, too. Six figure salary may not be worth it if you're not happy at the office.

3. Subjects you love

Some students choose a major simply because they love the subject matter. If you love what you're studying, you're more likely to fully engage with your classes and college experience, and that can mean better grades and great relationships with others in your field. If you love philosophy, don't write it off just because you're not sure about graduate school, or what the job market holds for philosophers. Many liberal arts majors provide students with critical thinking skills and writing abilities that are highly valued by employers.

4. Undecided? Explore your interests.

If you truly have no idea what you want to study, that's okay. Many schools don't require students to declare a major until sophomore year. That gives you four semesters to play the field. Make the most of any required general education courses, choose ones that interest you. Talk to professors, advisers, department heads, and other students. Find an internship off campus. Exploring your interests will help you find your best fit major, and maybe even your ideal career.

Can you change your mind? Definitely. One of the most exciting aspects of college life is that it introduces you to new subjects and fosters new passions. You might enter undergrad enjoying physics but discover a burgeoning love for political science. However, keep this in mind: every major has requisite coursework. Some require you to take introductory courses before you move into the more advanced classes. Also, some classes are offered in the fall but not in the spring, or vice versa. If you change your major late in the game, it may take you more than the traditional four years to earn a degree.

(495 words)

New words

*tuition	/tjuːˈɪʃn/	n.	学费
▲imperative	/ɪmˈperətɪv/	a.	必要的；势在必行的
prep	/prep/	n.	预备，准备
*specific	/spɪˈsɪfɪk/	a.	特定的；明确的
*relevant	/ˈreləvənt/	a.	相关的；贴切的；中肯的
▲discipline	/ˈdɪsəplɪn/	n.	学科
syllabus	/ˈsɪləbəs/	n.	教学大纲
*advanced	/ədˈvɑːnst/	a.	先进的；高级的
*seminar	/ˈsemɪnɑː/	n.	讨论会；研讨班
coursework	/ˈkɔːswɜːk/	n.	课程作业
*loan	/ləʊn/	n.	贷款
*statistics	/stəˈtɪstɪks/	n.	统计；统计学
▲economics	/ˌiːkəˈnɒmɪks/	n.	经济学
*figure	/ˈfɪɡə/	n.	数字
*critical	/ˈkrɪtɪkl/	a.	批评的；批判的
*explore	/ɪkˈsplɔː/	v.	探索；探究
*semester	/sɪˈmestə/	n.	学期
internship	/ˈɪntɜːnʃɪp/	n.	实习；实习岗位；（学生或毕业生的）实习期
▲definitely	/ˈdefɪnɪtli/	ad.	明确地；肯定地
*aspect	/ˈæspekt/	n.	方面
▲foster	/ˈfɒstə/	v.	促进；培养
*passion	/ˈpæʃn/	n.	激情；热情
undergrad	/ˈʌndəɡræd/	n.	大学（本科）生
burgeoning	/ˈbɜːdʒənɪŋ/	a.	迅速发展的；繁荣的
requisite	/ˈrekwɪzɪt/	a.	必备的，必不可少的

Phrases & expressions

check out	核实；查实
take out	取得，获得，领到（贷款、执照、保单等）
keep in mind	牢记；放在心上
be likely to do something	可能做……
engage with	忙于；从事
write off	注销；放弃
provide... with...	为……提供……
have no idea	对……一无所知
play the field	不专一；四处探索
make the most of	充分利用

vice versa	反之亦然
earn a degree	获得学位
day trader	做短线者；当日交易者
physical therapist	理疗师
web developer	网站开发员
actuarial mathematics	精算数学；保险统计数学
graduate school	研究生院
liberal arts	文科；人文科学
critical thinking	批判性思维
general education course	通识课程
introductory course	入门课程；基础课程

Proper names

PayScale.com	PayScale薪酬网（美国统计薪资收入的权威网站，拥有世界上最大、最完善的雇员薪酬数据库）

生词数	生词率	*B级词汇	*A级词汇	▲四、六级词汇	超纲词汇
26	5.25%	5	8	5	8

Notes

1. **college major**

    A college major is the area of study that a student will specialize in when pursuing a degree at a college or university. The choice of a major is the most important step a student makes. Some colleges do not let a student declare a major until the second year of college.

2. **PayScale.com**

    It is a website which empowers people and employers with fresh, transparent, and validated salary data, easy-to-use software, and services to get pay right under any market conditions.

3. **actuarial mathematics**

    Actuarial mathematics is the discipline that applies mathematical and statistical methods to assess risk in insurance, finance, and other industries and professions. More generally, actuaries apply rigorous mathematics to model matters of uncertainty.

4. **liberal arts**

    Liberal arts are college or university studies (such as language, philosophy, literature, abstract science) intended to provide chiefly general knowledge and to develop general intellectual capacities (such as reason and judgment) as opposed to professional or vocational skills.

Unit 1 | College Major Choices 7

After-reading tasks

Task 1 Tick off the factors to consider when choosing a major according to the passage.

☐ 1. college location   ☐ 2. career options

☐ 3. tuition & financial aid   ☐ 4. earning potential

☐ 5. subjects you love   ☐ 6. extracurricular activities

☐ 7. your interests   ☐ 8. college reputation

Task 2 Read the passage again and decide whether the following statements are true (T) or false (F). If it is false, write the key words to support your answer.

( ) 1. Major is different from career, so you don't need to prepare for the coursework required for your dream career.

_____

( ) 2. Future earning potential is a major factor for students to consider when choosing their majors.

_____

( ) 3. If you love your subjects, you're more likely to fully engage with your classes and get better grades and great relationships with people in this field.

_____

( ) 4. Sophomore year is definitely too late to choose a major.

_____

( ) 5. If you change your major very late, it may take more time to earn a degree.

_____

Listening and speaking

Task 1

Li Ming meets Wang Jie on the campus and they have a short talk on choosing a major. Wang Jie is also a freshman. They knew each other on the day they enrolled in the college. Listen to their conversation three times and choose the best answers to complete the following sentences.

1. This conversation most probably takes place _____.
   A. in the library   B. in a classroom   C. on the playground   D. not mentioned
2. Li Ming and Wang Jie have been college students for about _____.
   A. one month   B. one semester   C. one week   D. two weeks
3. So far _____ have helped Li Ming a lot in many aspects.
   A. freshmen   B. sophomores   C. juniors   D. seniors
4. It seems that Li Ming does not know how to _____.
   A. make new friends   B. find right classrooms   C. choose a major   D. finish assignments
5. Wang Jie does not recommend Li Ming to talk to _____ about choosing a major.
   A. freshmen   B. teachers from the Career Center
   C. juniors or seniors   D. friends

Unit 1 | College Major Choices

Task 2 Li Ming decides to seek help from the Career Center in his college. Mr. Wang, one of the advisers there, meets him warmly. Listen to their conversation three times and fill in the blanks.

Li Ming: Good morning, Mr. Wang.

Mr. Wang: Good morning, Li Ming.

Li Ming: Mr. Wang, I've got quite ___1___ at the names of some majors, and it makes me feel difficult to pick one as my major. Can you help me?

Mr. Wang: Sure, my pleasure and my duty. I ___2___ as a Career Counselor for more than 10 years. I can get information from different departments as well as ___3___.

Li Ming: Emm, Mr. Wang, what's the difference between the following two majors, Electronics & Information Technology, and Information Science Technology?

Mr. Wang: Well, you see, Electronics & Information Technology ___4___ electronic area and information technology, while Information Science Technology ___5___ information technology. They have different courses to support students to develop their ___6___. What's more, the ___7___ work in different industries, which means their ___8___ are different.

Li Ming: In your opinion, which one is easier?

Mr. Wang: They are different. It depends on your ___9___, learning involvement and ___10___.

Li Ming: Well, it seems I do need to think twice before making my decision.

Mr. Wang: Definitely.

Task 3 Mr. Wang also tells Li Ming about recommendations from alumni on some majors. Listen to his remarks three times and complete the following note.

Helpful source of information	• students _____ different areas of study; • students considering _____ major focus.
Valuable opinions about their major for	• college students; • _____ .
Majors generally recommended in	• science, _____ , _____ and mathematics.
Majors highly recommended in	• _____ , accounting and finance, _____ and health care management.
Majors seldom recommended in	• the arts, humanities and _____ .

Task 4 Li Ming is consulting Mrs. Song on how to choose a major. Listen to their conversation three times and tick off the items mentioned.

☐ 1. hobbies ☐ 2. alumni
☐ 3. salary and compensation ☐ 4. future job
☐ 5. personalities ☐ 6. graduate school
☐ 7. college major choice ☐ 8. future career development
☐ 9. critical thinking ☐ 10. the best college majors for the future

Task 5 Suppose you are Li Ming and your partner is a Career Counselor. You turn to him for advice on what major to choose. Make up a dialogue and role-play before your classmates.

Task 6 The following are four viewpoints concerning college major choice. Discuss them with your partner, and then tell each other which one you are for and why.

- Parents' suggestion is my first consideration for major choice.
- My personal interests determine my major choice.
- Career-related factors, such as job availability and employment rates, are the first considerations when I choose my major.
- I will surely consider my future income potential when picking a major.

Reading B

Li Ming is now at the Career Guidance Office, consulting about the best majors for the future. An office staff member shows him a report *The 6 best college majors for the future* **as below.**

The 6 best college majors for the future

People often say that the best college major should suit the person's interests. However, mere fondness for a particular field of study may not sustain the individual in the future. There are college majors that provide a more stable guarantee for the students' future careers. These best 6 college majors for the future hold promising career paths for students of today.

No. 6 Electrical engineering

Electrical engineering may not be an easy major, but it comes with high potential compensation and employment opportunities. Electrical engineers are in demand at power plants, large manufacturing facilities and other major companies. Their unemployment rate is between 5 to 7 percent with an average salary of around $60,000. The expected growth in employment for electrical engineers by 2020 is 6 percent.

No. 5 Construction management

Construction management is another college degree with increasing demand in employment. Construction managers are the ones who control building operations. Their unemployment rate only falls at about 5 percent, and their annual salary is around $50,000. The projected employment growth by 2020 is 17 percent.

No. 4 Nursing

Nurses have had a steady employment rate in the past years, and the fast-growing population of newborns and elderly people creates demand for more nurses. Nurses have a low unemployment rate of 4 percent and earn an average salary of $60,000. They are mostly in demand in hospitals and other healthcare facilities. The projected growth for their employment rate is 26 percent by 2020.

No. 3 Physical therapy

Obtaining a degree in physical therapy can be difficult. However, the end result is quite

rewarding for physical therapists. Physical therapists can find a lot of openings in hospitals and medical care centers. They have a low average unemployment of 2 to 5 percent. Their average salary is around $60,000 with a projected increase in employment of 33 percent by 2020.

No. 2 Aeronautics and aviation technology

Aeronautics and aviation technology poses great difficulties when it comes to academics. However, graduates in this field of study earn a good salary with excellent growth opportunities. People who work for airlines and airplane manufacturers make an average salary of $60,000 and above. Their unemployment rate is only 4 percent with an expected growth of 5 percent by 2020.

No. 1 Pharmacology

Among the highest earners are people with degrees in pharmacology. Pharmacists are often in demand in pharmacies and hospitals. They earn an average salary of $105,000 depending on their degree level and experience. Their unemployment rate falls at a low 3 percent with projected growth of 25 percent in employment by 2020.

(425 words)

New words

*mere	/mɪə(r)/	a.	仅仅的
▲sustain	/səˈsteɪn/	v.	使维持
*stable	/ˈsteɪbl/	a.	稳定的
▲guarantee	/ˌɡærənˈtiː/	n.	保证；担保
▲promising	/ˈprɒmɪsɪŋ/	a.	有前途的；有希望的
▲compensation	/ˌkɒmpenˈseɪʃn/	n.	薪酬；报酬；赔偿（金）
*facility	/fəˈsɪləti/	n.	设施；设备
*annual	/ˈænjuəl/	a.	每年的；一年一次的
*project	/prəˈdʒekt/	v.	规划；估计
*obtain	/əbˈteɪn/	v.	获得；得到
▲rewarding	/rɪˈwɔːdɪŋ/	a.	值得做的；有益的
▲therapist	/ˈθerəpɪst/	n.	治疗专家
aeronautics	/ˌeərəˈnɔːtɪks/	n.	航空学
▲aviation	/ˌeɪviˈeɪʃn/	n.	航空
▲pose	/pəʊz/	v.	造成（威胁、问题等）；提问
▲academics	/ˌækəˈdemɪks/	n.	学习；学术
*airline	/ˈeəlaɪn/	n.	航空公司
pharmacology	/ˌfɑːməˈkɒlədʒi/	n.	药物学；药理学
pharmacist	/ˈfɑːməsɪst/	n.	药剂师

Phrases & expressions

suit one's interests	适合某人的兴趣
fondness for	喜爱……
in demand	很受欢迎；需求量大
when it comes to	一谈到……；当提到……时
field of study	专业领域；研究领域
power plants	发电厂
unemployment rate	失业率
average salary	平均工资
college degree	大学学位
employment rate	就业率
airplane manufacturers	飞机制造商

生词数	生词率	*B级词汇	*A级词汇	▲四、六级词汇	超纲词汇
19	4.47%	4	2	10	3

Notes

1. **electrical engineering**

   Electrical engineering is the branch of engineering science that studies the uses of electricity, the equipment for power generation and distribution, and the control of machines and communication.

2. **pharmacology**

   Pharmacology is the science of drugs including their origin, composition, pharmaceutics, therapeutic use, and toxicology, and the properties and reactions of drugs especially with reaction to their therapeutic value.

 After-reading tasks

Task 1 Complete the following table with the information taken from the passage.

College Major	Corresponding Job	Unemployment Rate	Average Salary	Expected Employment Growth by 2020
Electrical Engineering	electrical engineer		around $60,000	6 percent
Construction Management		about 5 percent	$50,000	17 percent
Nursing	nurse	4 percent	$60,000	
Physical Therapy		2 to 5 percent	$60,000	33 percent
	————	4 percent	$60,000	5 percent
Pharmacology	pharmacist	3 percent		25 percent

Task 2 Translate the following paragraph into Chinese.

Electrical engineering may not be an easy major, but it comes with high potential compensation and employment opportunities. Electrical engineers are in demand at power plants, large manufacturing facilities and other major companies. Their unemployment rate is between 5 to 7 percent with an average salary of around $60,000. The expected growth in employment for electrical engineers by 2020 is 6 percent.

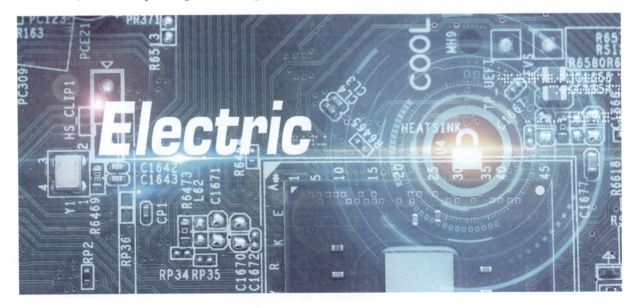

Comprehensive exercises

Task 1 Fill in the blanks with the words or expressions from Readings A and B according to the meanings in the right column. The first letter of each word is already given to help your spelling. Then compare your answers with your partner.

c_____	to look for faults; to point out faults
r_____	needed for a particular purpose
f_____	to encourage (something) to grow or develop
r_____	connected with the subject
s_____	to continue for some time without becoming less
p_____	to create a threat, problem, etc. that has to be dealt with
t_____	to get something officially
c_____	to test, examine, or mark to see if something is correct
e_____	to get involved with and try to understand something or somebody
w_____	to regard as being lost, having lost, etc.

Task 2 Complete the following sentences with the words and expressions from Task 1. Change the form if necessary.

1. Though her speech lasted very long, she managed to _____ everyone's interest until the end of it.
2. We had to _____ our new projects because it was impossible for us to find the capital for them in just three weeks.
3. Immediately after the serious traffic accident, the policemen questioned tens of passers-by to _____ whether the driver had told a true story.
4. It has been widely accepted that students should be encouraged to develop _____ thinking instead of accepting opinions without questioning them.
5. She lacks the _____ experience for the job, which is really a weak point for her application.
6. The Johnsons didn't have enough money to buy a new apartment, so they planned to _____ a loan from the local bank.
7. The freshmen were told that a question-and-answer meeting would be held tonight, and all people present could _____ questions concerning major choice.
8. Surprisingly, Mrs. Taylor had the ability to _____ young minds though she was born a generation ago.
9. The club has made it very clear that its aim is to _____ better relations within the community.
10. Generally speaking, where you come from isn't _____ to whether you will become a top student or not.

Task 3 Complete the following sentences with the appropriate forms of the words given in the brackets.

1. Most countries were facing an economic crisis in 2008, and the _____ (employ) rate reached a very high level worldwide.
2. Mary is very _____ (like) to pass the final exam, for she has been working very hard during the past two months.
3. Last night, the Labor Union declared that the strike would not stop unless the _____ (manage) agreed to raise their basic salary.
4. Franklin dreams to become a physical _____ (therapy) so that he can help his parents to raise their big family.
5. Even when she was a little girl, Sophia had a strong _____ (fond) for volleyball.
6. The world began to regard cultural industry as the most _____ (promise) industry from the early 1990s.
7. Her aunts strongly asked her to choose education as her major, because they thought a lot of _____ (open) could be found in schools of all levels.
8. The USA has remained as the most _____ (advance) industrial country for more than two centuries.
9. It will be much better to take some _____ (introduce) courses before you make up your mind to give birth to a child next year.
10. We think it a must for modern college students to develop critical _____ (think) if they want to take on more responsibilities in the future.

Task 4 Rewrite the following sentences according to the examples.

Example 1: Make sure you're ready for the coursework *which/that is required for the career of your dreams*.
→Make sure you're ready for the coursework *required for the career of your dreams*.

1. The novel which was bought yesterday was really very moving.

2. The bridge that was built several years ago was swept away by the heavy flood.

3. You will have to prepare all the things that are needed for this long journey.

4. We had a heated discussion about those measures that had been taken to deal with financial difficulties.

5. Many people in North Canada still follow some old traditions that have been passed down to modern times.

Unit 1 | College Major Choices

Example 2: If you change your major late in the game, *you will spend more than the traditional four years earning a degree.*
→If you change your major late in the game, *it may take you more than the traditional four years to earn a degree.*

1. Jim spent about three months in getting a driver's license.

2. Karl spent a whole day in reviewing all the lessons he had learned this semester.

3. They spent a lot of time in explaining the new plan to their co-workers.

4. The drawer has spent about ten years learning to draw a beautiful horse in five minutes.

5. Millions of brave Chinese spent nearly half a century founding the People's Republic of China.

Task 5 Complete the following English sentences using the words or phrases given in the brackets.

1. Since you have chosen this major, you should try to _____ _____ (培养成为一名优秀理疗师的热情). (foster, passion, physical therapist)

2. They _____ (不得不取消一些必要的讨论会) because the time was very limited. (write off, requisite, seminar)

3. Before you decide on your major, _____ _____ (有必要核实一下要交多少学费). (imperative, check out, tuition)

4. _____ (我们大学生应当牢记，获得学位至关重要), and so is to develop critical thinking. (keep in mind, earn a degree)

5. _____ (经理为他提供了许多机会), but it's really a pity that _____ (他却对此一无所知). (provide... with..., have no idea)

Applied writing

通知

通知是运用广泛的知照性公文,即在某件事情将要发生之前告知相关信息的简短公文。通知往往包含一些重要信息,如通知的事件、该事件将要发生的具体时间、发布通知的日期及发布通知的人员。阅读下面的通知样例,并指出其中的重要信息。

Sample

Notice

In order to make our school life colorful and improve our English skills, we're going to hold an English Play Show in the meeting room, No. 2 Teaching Building at 8:00 p.m. this Saturday, April 10th. At the English Play Show, we can not only enjoy English plays and speeches, but also sing English songs and play English games. What's more, our foreign teacher Mr. Taylor will give a talk about how to improve oral English. I hope everyone who comes here will have a great time. If you'd like to come, please sign your name at the Students' Union, Room 203, Office Building.

April 7th, 2010
Students' Union

✏ Writing task

In order to help freshmen like Li Ming to make choices, the Students' Union plans to hold a seminar on *How to choose a major*. You are required to write a notice according to the Chinese information given below.

讲座时间：2021年9月15日（星期三）下午2点至4点
讲座地点：教学楼4103室
主 讲 人：就业指导中心主任余教授
通知日期：2021年9月9日

❋ Words for reference

1. Career Guidance Center 就业指导中心
2. Teaching Building 教学楼
3. lecture 讲座

Project performing

Guidelines

This project aims to simulate relevant situations of choosing a college major. The whole task is divided into three steps. Step one is about trying to find those factors that should be considered. Step two focuses on persons that can be turned to for advice. Step three is concerned with making a final decision.

Please follow the task description to complete the project.

Task description

Step one

- Organize a small group of 4 to 6 students in your class;
- Brainstorm and share the factors that have some influence on your major choices;
- Give a presentation to introduce the factors that all group members consider very important when choosing a major.

Step two

- List as many people as possible that you may ask for advice on major choice;
- Divide the group into two sides: One side is advice-seekers, the other is advice-givers;
- Take turns to play roles: The side of advice-seekers tries to get advice, and the other side asks for information on advice-seekers' ideal future jobs.

Step three

- The side of advice-seekers writes notes on at least 5 future jobs, and the side of advice-givers writes notes on at least 5 pieces of advice accordingly;
- Discuss each piece of advice with reference to corresponding future jobs;
- Give a presentation to the whole class about your final choice and give your reason(s).

Grammar

名词复数的变化形式

1. 规则变化：名词的复数一般在名词词尾加-s或-es构成

类别	构成法	单数	复数
一般情况	加-s	map cat tub	maps cats tubs
以字母s, x, ch, sh结尾的词	加-es	box class watch brush	boxes classes watches brushes
以字母o结尾的词	加-es或-s	potato hero bamboo studio	potatoes heroes bamboos studios
以"辅音字母+y"结尾的词	把y改成i，再加-es	factory story	factories stories
以字母f或fe结尾的词	把f或fe改为v，再加es	shelf knife	shelves knives

2. 不规则变化：名词的复数存在许多不规则的变化形式

构成法	单数/复数		
改变内部元音	foot—feet man—men	goose—geese woman—women	tooth—teeth mouse—mice
词尾加-en或ren	ox—oxen	child—children	
单复数形式相同	sheep—sheep	deer—deer	fish—fish　　Chinese—Chinese

3. 名词单数和复数的特殊用法

特殊用法	例词/例句
有些名词单数和复数的意义不同	air/airs（空气/神气），content/contents（内容/目录），custom/customs（习惯/海关），fish/fishes（鱼/鱼的种类），glass/glasses（玻璃/眼镜），step/steps（脚步/台阶），work/works（工作/作品）
有些名词虽然以-s结尾，但在句中做主语时，谓语动词用单数。如：news, Athens（雅典），Brussels（布鲁塞尔）	The news on TV is always depressing. Athens has grown rapidly in the past decade.
以-s结尾表示学科的名词在句中做主语时，谓语动词用单数	Mathematics is a compulsory subject at school.

Task 1 Choose the best answer to complete each of the following sentences.

1. He has done many _____.
   A. work B. job C. works D. jobs

2. There _____ on the wall, they are very nice.
   A. are photos B. are photoes C. is a photo D. is photo

3. A cat has four _____, doesn't it?
   A. A. foots B. feets C. foot D. feet

4. Maths _____ the language of science.
   A. are B. is C. have D. has

5. No news _____ good news.
   A. are B. is C. have D. has

6. The _____ are searching our bags.
   A. custom officer B. customs officer C. customs officers D. custom officers

7. Economics _____ only recently been recognized as a scientific study.
   A. are B. is C. has D. have

8. You'll see many kinds of _____ in the fish market.
   A. fish B. fishes C. a fish D. some fishes

9. My uncle has three _____.
   A. child B. childs C. children D. childrens

10. They are _____.
    A. woman teachers B. women teachers C. women teacher D. woman teacher

Unit 1 | College Major Choices

Task 2 Complete the following sentences with the proper forms of the given nouns.

1. I don't like _____ (fly, flys, flies) because they are ugly and dirty.
2. These _____ (boy, boys, boies) like _____ (monkey, monkeys, monkeies).
3. Brush your _____ (tooth, teeth), Kitty. It's time for bed.
4. There are many _____ (animal, animals) in the zoo. I like _____ (giraffe, giraffes).
5. There are four _____ (Japanese, Japaneses) and two _____ (German, Germen, Germans) in the group.
6. A pair of _____ (glass, glasses) costs quite a lot these days.
7. The _____ (stair, stairs) are quite narrow, so be careful when you go down.
8. The boy has two _____ (watch, watches, watchs).
9. _____ (Politic, Politics) is popular at this university.
10. They come from different _____ (country, countries, countrys).

Task 3 Write down the plural forms of the following nouns.

1. orange _____	2. class _____	3. text _____
4. church _____	5. piano _____	6. lady _____
7. Chinese _____	8. goose _____	9. toy _____
10. dish _____	11. shelf _____	12. fox _____
13. radio _____	14. hero _____	15. mouse _____

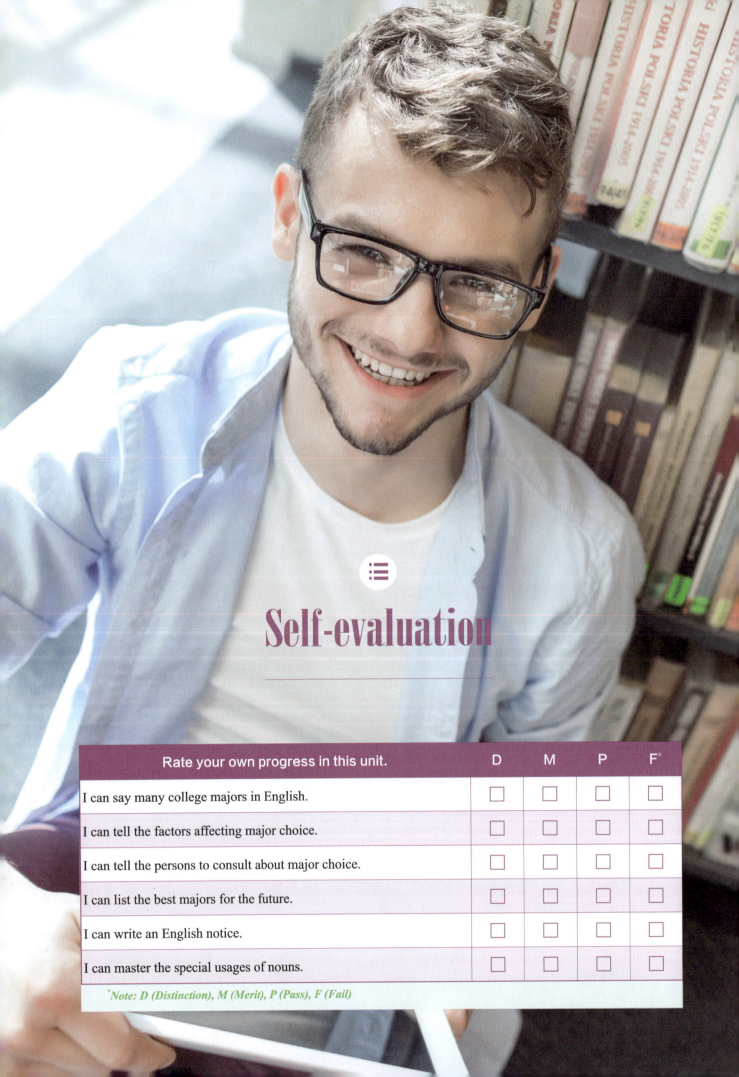

Self-evaluation

Rate your own progress in this unit.	D	M	P	F*
I can say many college majors in English.	☐	☐	☐	☐
I can tell the factors affecting major choice.	☐	☐	☐	☐
I can tell the persons to consult about major choice.	☐	☐	☐	☐
I can list the best majors for the future.	☐	☐	☐	☐
I can write an English notice.	☐	☐	☐	☐
I can master the special usages of nouns.	☐	☐	☐	☐

*Note: D (Distinction), M (Merit), P (Pass), F (Fail)

Unit 1 | College Major Choices

Culture

教育是就业之基，就业是民生之本。授人以鱼，不如授人以渔。职业教育是广大青年打开成功成才大门的重要途径，具有培养多样化人才、传承技术技能、促进就业创业的重要作用。政府数据分析显示，"十三五"期间，我国职业教育取得丰硕成果，其中一大亮点是在服务脱贫攻坚中发挥了重要作用。

来自贫困家庭的陈招娣通过国家免费职业教育计划和自身的努力圆了自己的求学就业梦，此后将有更多的年轻人从中受益，实现个人和家庭命运的转变。

 Task 1 Watch the following video clip, and then read the script imitating the pronunciation and intonation.

Twenty-three-year-old Chen Zhaodi is a housekeeping manager for a hotel in Qingyuan City. She got the job after graduating from college four months ago and she is quite satisfied with it. She's also grateful to her school, as three years ago it seemed poverty has destroyed her chance of studying. "I burst into tears when I enrolled as I had almost given up hope of studying. My family couldn't afford my tuition for my higher education, so I applied for a charity vocational college. It was my last chance and I got it!"

This is the school that changes Chen's life. Actually it is China's first vocational school providing free education for students coming from impoverished areas. Founded by a businessman in 2014, the vocational college now has a thousand students. It offers seven majors related to hotel management, construction and preschool education, besides tuition the college also provides accommodation and covers living expenses. The school says, "Students don't need to pay a penny but they are expected to study hard." "We believe the best way to help families out of poverty is to educate their children. We teach them skills and help them find decent jobs to prevent poverty from passing down to the next generation."

Task 2 Discuss the following topics in groups.

1. Do you have any idea of the national policies towards students from impoverished families during higher education?
2. List majors that are the good ones for students and families out of impoverished areas to choose from.

Unit 2
Autonomous Learning

Learning objectives

After studying this unit, you should be able to:
- get familiar with the words and expressions concerning study plan;
- know the importance of autonomous learning for future education;
- have some idea of how to manage time more effectively;
- be clear about how to make a good study plan;
- master the skills of writing a timetable;
- be expert at the special usages of adjectives and adverbs.

Warm-up

Task 1 Watch the video that shows you the answers to the following questions. Then try to answer them orally. Some key words and phrases are listed for you.

specific 具体的　　realistic 现实的　　measurable 可测量的
time-bound 有时限的　　acceptable 可接受的　　agenda 议事日程

1. What are the SMART principles developed by Edwin Locke in 1981 for making a good study plan?
2. How can you start using the SMART theory?
3. What questions can you ask to check for all study activities if they are SMART?

Task 2 Read this study plan, then answer the following questions.

1. Which periods of time are for study group, lecture and exam?
2. Which periods of time are for the planned social appointments?
3. Which periods of time are for relaxation/free times?
4. Which periods of time are for the self-study?

Reading A

During the orientation week, all the freshmen are organized to attend a lecture about autonomous learning. Li Ming raises a few questions at the end of the lecture. The lecturer recommends Li Ming to read an article entitled *Autonomous learning is the future of education* as below.

Pre-reading questions

1. What is autonomous learning?
2. What should students do in an autonomous classroom?

Autonomous learning is the future of education

We live in an exciting age of innovation. Technology plays an enormous role in that innovative spirit of change and discovery. Probably one of the most talked about technologies in today's world is the self-driving car. Just think of the possibilities a driverless car presents: reading the newspaper on the way to work, getting your workout on the exercise machine installed in the car, watching the news on TV, and the list goes on and on. Could this be our future? Some say, "Why do we need a self-driving car? My car gets me where I want to go." Future-ready thinkers say, "Why not?"

We are presented with the same kind of thinking when it comes to education. Let's think about the self-driving student, also known as the self-directed learner or the autonomous learner. What do we mean by autonomous learning? Autonomous learning can be referred to as student-centered learning, shifting the focus of education from teaching to learning.

The teaching curriculum might look a bit different in the autonomous classroom. The teacher will be responsible for sharing self-monitoring strategies. Students might use learning logs or charts and tables to follow their progress. Teachers will teach error analysis and help students use their mistakes as learning opportunities to accommodate their learning goals. Teachers must provide the necessary guidance to help students choose their personal learning goals. Teachers must provide feedback as students pursue their own questions and solve their own problems. Teachers remain the most important part of the autonomous classroom.

Let's take a look at autonomous learning: The student is working on his science objective in the field of chemistry. He goes into his virtual science laboratory. Here he experiments using chemicals that might be considered dangerous in the traditional classroom. In his virtual lab, the student witnesses the chemical reactions and must determine why the chemical reacted in that manner. While in that virtual world, he finds an artificially intelligent computer that moves the student through a lesson on chemical reactions. The student then logs his work and determines his ability to meet his goals. He then meets in a small discussion group with his teacher and others to solve real world problems using necessary math skills. After making a determination and deriving at a solution, the teacher uses augmented reality (AR) to determine if their solution actually solved the problem. The student will continue his learning at home as he uses his foreign language application to practice his chosen foreign language as he prepares to meet his "Family Abroad".

Autonomous learning is the future of education. We must now think that instead of having a classroom of twenty students, we now have "twenty classrooms" of one student, each with their own agenda.

(470 words)

New words

▲autonomous	/ɔːˈtɒnəməs/	a.	自主的；自发的
▲innovation	/ˌɪnəˈveɪʃn/	n.	创新，革新
▲innovative	/ˈɪnəveɪtɪv/	a.	创新的
*enormous	/ɪˈnɔːməs/	a.	巨大的
*possibility	/ˌpɒsəˈbɪləti/	n.	可能性
*present	/prɪˈzent/	v.	展现；描述
▲workout	/ˈwɜːkaʊt/	n.	锻炼；健身
*install	/ɪnˈstɔːl/	v.	安装
*shift	/ʃɪft/	v.	转移；变换
▲curriculum	/kəˈrɪkjələm/	n.	课程
*log	/lɒg/	n.	日志
		v.	把……载入日志

*error	/ˈerə(r)/	n.	误差；错误
▲accommodate	/əˈkɒmədeɪt/	v.	使适应
*guidance	/ˈgaɪdns/	n.	指导；引导
*feedback	/ˈfiːdbæk/	n.	反馈
*pursue	/pəˈsjuː/	v.	从事；追求
*objective	/əbˈdʒektɪv/	n.	目标
*virtual	/ˈvɜːtʃuəl/	a.	虚拟的
*witness	/ˈwɪtnəs/	v.	目击；见证
artificially	/ˌɑːtəˈfɪʃəli/	ad.	人工地（人造地、人为地）；不自然地
*intelligent	/ɪnˈtelɪdʒənt/	a.	智能的；有智力的
▲reaction	/riˈækʃn/	n.	反应
▲determine	/dɪˈtɜːmɪn/	v.	决定
▲manner	/ˈmænə(r)/	n.	方式
▲derive	/dɪˈraɪv/	v.	源于；获得
▲augment	/ɔːgˈment/	v.	增加；增大
*application	/ˌæplɪˈkeɪʃn/	n.	应用程序
*agenda	/əˈdʒendə/	n.	议程；日程表

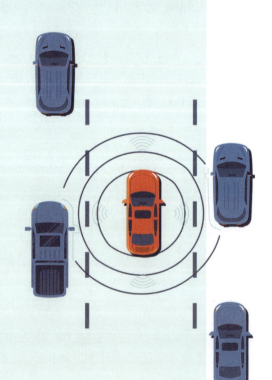

💬 Phrases & expressions

refer to	指的是
work on	致力于，从事于
move through	完成；穿过
derive at	得出
innovative spirit	创新精神
self-driving car	自动驾驶汽车
driverless car	无人驾驶汽车
future-ready thinkers	面向未来的思想家
self-driving student	自我驱动的学生
self-directed learner	自主学习者
autonomous learning	自主学习
student-centered learning	以学生为中心的学习
teaching curriculum	教学课程
autonomous classroom	自主学习课堂
self-monitoring strategy	自我监控策略
error analysis	失误分析
chemical reaction	化学反应
augmented reality	增强现实

生词数	生词率	*B级词汇	*A级词汇	▲四、六级词汇	超纲词汇
31	5.96%	8	8	11	1

Notes

1. self-driving car

A self-driving car, also known as an autonomous vehicle, a driverless car, is a vehicle that is capable of sensing its environment and moving safely with little or no human input.

2. autonomous classroom

An autonomous classroom is a class where the teacher is able to give more attention to high-level learning instead of spending all of their time repeating simple instructions, or solving problems that students can solve on their own.

3. artificial intelligence

Artificial intelligence (AI) makes it possible for machines to learn from experience, adjust to new inputs and perform human-like tasks. Most AI examples that you hear about today—from chess-playing computers to self-driving cars—rely heavily on deep learning and natural language processing. Using these technologies, computers can be trained to accomplish specific tasks by processing large amounts of data and recognizing patterns in the data.

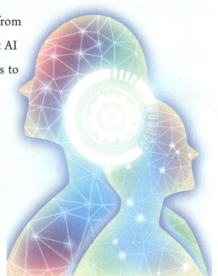

4. augmented reality

Augmented reality (AR) is an enhanced version of the real physical world that is achieved through the use of digital visual elements, sound, or other sensory stimuli delivered via technology.

After-reading tasks

Task 1 Read the passage and fill in the blanks with the appropriate information from the passage.

Autonomous learning can be referred to as ___1___ learning, shifting the focus of education from ___2___ to learning. In the autonomous classroom, the teacher is responsible for sharing self-monitoring strategies. ___3___ use learning logs or charts and tables to follow their progress. Teachers provide the necessary guidance to help students choose their personal ___4___. Teachers must provide ___5___ as students pursue their own questions and solve their own problems. Teachers remain the most important part of the autonomous classroom.

Task 2 Read the passage again and decide whether the following statements are true (T) or false (F). If it is false, write the key words to support your answer.

( ) 1. The driverless car is our future and everyone needs it.
___

( ) 2. Autonomous learning is student-centered, so students are the most important part of the autonomous classroom.
___

( ) 3. In the autonomous classroom, students can use their mistakes as learning opportunities to accommodate their learning goals.
___

( ) 4. In a virtual lab, students can experiment with chemicals that might be considered dangerous in the traditional classroom.
___

( ) 5. Students cannot use an artificially intelligent computer to learn a chemical lesson.
___

Listening and speaking

Task 1 Li Ming is deeply impressed by the lecture and the article above about autonomous learning during the orientation week. He talks about it with Mrs. Song during the class break. Mrs. Song shares with him what autonomous learning means. Listen to her words three times and complete the following note.

Autonomous learning means that students can	• _____ their learning _____.
Students can set their goals by	• _____ a list of goals to know where to begin their learning process.
The second benefit is	• knowing their learning _____.
The third benefit is	• placing _____ on progress; • paying much attention to learning _____.
In autonomous learning students get support to	• keep their _____; • improve their _____ skills.

Task 2 Li Ming thinks Mrs. Song's words are very impressive. After the class, he continues to consult her on how to find his own learning style. Listen to their conversation three times and choose the best answers to complete the following sentences.

1. This conversation most probably takes place _____.
   A. in the office   B. in a classroom   C. on the playground   D. in the library
2. For auditory learners, they learn by _____.
   A. hearing and listening   B. reading and seeing
   C. touching and doing   D. reading and touching
3. For visual learners, they learn by _____.
   A. hearing and listening   B. reading and seeing
   C. touching and doing   D. hearing and touching
4. For tactile learners, they learn by _____.
   A. hearing and listening   B. reading and seeing
   C. touching and doing   D. listening and seeing
5. Mrs. Song asks Li Ming to _____ what learning activities he tends to prefer.
   A. design   B. test   C. comment on   D. reflect on

Task 3 Recently, Li Ming finds it hard to deal with his study and worries a lot about the coming exams. His friend Wang Jie gives him some advice on time management. Listen to their conversation three times and fill in the blanks.

Wang Jie: Hello, Li Ming! How are you?

Li Ming: I am fine, Wang Jie. But I am a little worried about my exams. They are going to start and I have little ___1___.

Wang Jie: Why haven't you prepared well for your exams?

Li Ming: I could not find time to prepare. I have been busy in my football match and writing my book.

Wang Jie: Oh! That's not ___2___. You must have ___3___ time for your studies.

Li Ming: I could not realize the ___4___ of time and I have wasted a lot.

Wang Jie: So, now what is your plan?

Li Ming: I am worried how I can study all the courses in this short period of time.

Wang Jie: You must make a ___5___ for study. Decide the most ___6___ things and give some time to them.

Li Ming: I have just 20 days left. I have to prepare all the three subjects.

Wang Jie: So, get relaxed. Just ___7___ important content and prepare it well.

Li Ming: Can you give me some advice on time management?

Wang Jie: Yes. The first thing is to set up a ___8___ for your daily activities. Try to do all those in the time period you've given. That is the only way you can get the things well going on.

Li Ming: OK. I will try to do this.

Wang Jie: Also give time to all activities according to their importance. For example, now your studies are the ___9___ to do, so give more time to it. ___10___ the activities that are of little importance. There your football match has ended and there is no need to give time to sports regularly.

Li Ming: Oh! That is a really great idea. I hope now I can do something to get through the exams.

Wang Jie: Good. Best of luck with your exams. I have to go now. Goodbye!

Li Ming: Thanks. How nice of you! Goodbye!

Task 4 Li Ming finally gets through his exams. He feels lucky this time but he knows he cannot be lucky all the time. He decides to consult Mrs. Song again on how to make a good study plan. Listen to their conversation three times and tick off the items mentioned.

- [ ] 1. keep a to-do list
- [ ] 2. make a timetable
- [ ] 3. decide high-importance tasks
- [ ] 4. make a note of the difficult tasks
- [ ] 5. decide low-importance tasks
- [ ] 6. write the time for the task
- [ ] 7. tick those I've done
- [ ] 8. make a note of the most important tasks
- [ ] 9. cross off those I've done
- [ ] 10. set some notes to remind me of the schedule

Task 5 Suppose you are Li Ming and your partner is good at time management. You turn to him for advice on managing time. Make up a dialogue and role-play before your classmates.

Task 6 The following are four viewpoints concerning autonomous learning. Discuss them with your partner, and then tell each other which one you can do, and which one you cannot do and why not.

- The autonomous learners take responsibility for their own learning, set goals, control progress, and understand what they have mastered.
- The autonomous learners can make their own decisions with the aim of achieving their personal goals.
- In autonomous learning, students should be aware of their own learning styles.
- In autonomous learning, students need to develop their own learning methods.

Reading B

Li Ming is now in the library, reading the article *How to create a study plan*, which he got from Mrs. Song. He hopes to make his own study plan after reading it.

How to create a study plan

It's important to understand that there is no "right" way to make a study plan. Your study plan will be personalized based on your specific needs, classes, and learning style.

Follow the guidelines below to get started on creating your study plan:

#1: Analyze your current study habits and learning style. Think about what works and what doesn't work for you. Are you able to study for long blocks of time once or twice a week, or is it more effective if you study nightly for thirty minutes? Are you more productive at a certain time of day? Do you retain material better if you study a subject immediately after class, or do you need a break first?

#2: Evaluate your current schedule and time management. Use a digital or paper calendar to block out all of your standing commitments, including classes, work, and extracurricular activities. This will let you see how much of your time is already spoken for, and what time you have available for studying. If your schedule leaves little room for studying, you may need to evaluate what you can cut back on, or how you can rearrange your schedule to have more open time for studying.

#3: Plan how much time you need to study for each class. At the beginning of each term, your instructors will give you syllabi for the classes you are taking. The syllabi will usually include the dates of any major exams or projects. You can use these as guides for calculating how much time to set aside for each class, as some courses might be more intensive than others. It will also help you schedule your study sessions to make sure you have enough time to complete all your assignments and prepare for exams.

#4: Develop a schedule. Now that you understand how much time you need for studying, and how much time you have available, you can schedule your study sessions. Add your study sessions to your calendar like any other commitments. This ensures that you remember this is time set aside specifically for studying.

#5: Assess your weekly calendar. At the beginning of each week, determine why you need to study and what you plan to accomplish in each study session. Are you preparing for a big exam? Is there a paper due? Are you able to read a chapter ahead in preparation for the next few classes? Adjust your study plan as necessary to meet your weekly goals, and get the most out of each study session.

#6: Stick to your schedule. A study plan works best when it is followed consistently. You should try to develop a study plan that you can follow for the length of each term. You will have to adjust your plan as necessary when you switch your classes each term. Remember, the most important thing is sticking to your plan.

(434 words)

New words

personalize	/ˈpɜːsənəlaɪz/	vt.	使个性化
*analyze	/ˈænəlaɪz/	vt.	对……进行分析
*current	/ˈkʌrənt/	a.	现在的
*effective	/ɪˈfektɪv/	a.	有效的,起作用的
▲productive	/prəˈdʌktɪv/	a.	富有成效的
*retain	/rɪˈteɪn/	vt.	保持;记住
*evaluate	/ɪˈvæljueɪt/	vt.	评价;估价
▲digital	/ˈdɪdʒɪtl/	a.	数字的
*calendar	/ˈkælɪndə(r)/	n.	日历;记事本
▲standing	/ˈstændɪŋ/	a.	长期存在的;永久性的;常设的
▲commitment	/kəˈmɪtmənt/	n.	不得不做的事
*available	/əˈveɪləbl/	a.	可获得的
*rearrange	/ˌriːəˈreɪndʒ/	vt.	重新排列
▲instructor	/ɪnˈstrʌktə(r)/	n.	教员;指导者
syllabi	/ˈsɪləbaɪ/	n.	摘要(syllabus的复数)
*calculate	/ˈkælkjuleɪt/	vi.	计算
▲intensive	/ɪnˈtensɪv/	a.	加强的;集中的
*assignment	/əˈsaɪnmənt/	n.	作业;功课
▲specifically	/spəˈsɪfɪkli/	ad.	特别地;明确地
*assess	/əˈses/	v.	对……进行评估
*accomplish	/əˈkʌmplɪʃ/	vt.	完成;实现
▲due	/djuː/	a.	到期的
*adjust	/əˈdʒʌst/	vt.	调整,使……适合
▲consistently	/kənˈsɪstəntli/	ad.	一贯地
*switch	/swɪtʃ/	v.	替换;转换

Phrases & expressions

base on	基于……；以……为根据
get started on	开始做
block out	挡住；遮挡
speak for	预定得到……；占用
leave little room for	几乎没有留下空间
cut back on	削减；缩减
set aside	留出
add… to	增加；增添
get the most out of	充分利用；发挥……的最大功效
stick to	坚持……
learning style	学习方式；学习风格
study habits	学习习惯
blocks of time	整块时间
extracurricular activity	课外活动
study session	学习时间（段）

生词数	生词率	*B级词汇	*A级词汇	▲四、六级词汇	超纲词汇
25	5.76%	5	9	9	2

After-reading tasks

Task 1 Match the English phrases in the left column with their Chinese equivalents in the right column.

( ) 1. extracurricular activities   A. 挡住；遮挡
( ) 2. cut back on   B. 充分利用；发挥……最大功效
( ) 3. study session   C. 削减；缩减
( ) 4. base on   D. 学习方式
( ) 5. block out   E. 预定得到……；占用
( ) 6. set aside   F. 基于……；以……为根据
( ) 7. get the most out of   G. 坚持……
( ) 8. speak for   H. 学习时间（段）
( ) 9. stick to   I. 留出
( ) 10. learning style   J. 课外活动

Task 2 Translate the following paragraph into Chinese.

Evaluate your current schedule and time management. Use a digital or paper calendar to block out all of your standing commitments, including classes, work, and extracurricular activities. This will let you see how much of your time is already spoken for, and what time you have available for studying. If your schedule leaves little room for studying, you may need to evaluate what you can cut back on, or how you can rearrange your schedule to have more open time for studying.

Comprehensive exercises

Task 1 Fill in the blanks with the words or expressions from Readings A and B according to the meanings in the right column. The first letter of each word is already given to help your spelling. Then compare your answers with your partner.

i_____	to fix equipment into position so that it can be used
a_____	to consider something when deciding what to do
p_____	to make efforts to achieve it, often over a long period of time
e_____	to form an opinion of the amount, value or quality of somebody/something after careful thinking
a_____	to be successful in doing something
s_____	to ask for a thing or a person, so no one else can have them
r_____	to use a particular word, expression, or name to mention or describe something
b_____	to keep a period of time for someone or something
b_____	to develop or found something, such as one's ideas or attitude on something else
s_____	to continue doing rather than changing to something else

Task 2 Complete the following sentences with the words and expressions from Task 1. Change the form if necessary.

1. As a modern college student, your primary education goal is to _____ knowledge and skills.
2. The term "time machine", invented by Wells, is now generally used to _____ a bus, a car or a truck that takes people into the far future.
3. Dieting and exercising can bring your weight under control but you must _____ your plan without changing your mind even for a second.
4. Having to _____ a different App for each smart appliance in your home will make you a bit angry; it would be nicer if you could manage everything together.
5. Jerry asked Nancy if she was willing to be his girlfriend, not knowing that Nancy had already _____.
6. It is wise for the employer not to _____ a job applicant according to his/her appearance but to his/her capabilities and work experiences.
7. When people always feel under pressure, they will find ways to _____ that pressure, including changing their schedules and work habits.
8. I'll accept anxiety as another name for challenge, and I believe by working hard I can _____ wonders.
9. Employers make many hiring decisions _____ the working experience of job applicants, which is not good news for fresh graduates.
10. To be full of energy for work in the daytime, you'd better _____ seven or eight hours for sleep every night.

Task 3 Complete the following sentences with the appropriate forms of the words given in the brackets.

1. The article says many people tend to think that _____ (innovative) just means creating something new, but actually it's more than that.
2. This little child is too young to worry about the _____ (possible) that sweets are harmful to his teeth.
3. Today's teenagers respect their parents and welcome parental _____ (guide) about important matters such as career choice.
4. Being responsible for law and order, the police is demanded to make quick _____ (act) to a potentially dangerous situation.
5. His _____ (determine) remains as strong as ever despite all the difficulties he has met.
6. It's important to _____ (personal) the gift with some Chinese elements, which will make people a deeper impression on Chinese culture.
7. Going to college means a new stage of life, and the students have many _____ (commit) including becoming autonomous learners.

8. Recent studies show that we are far more _____ (produce) at work if we take short breaks regularly.
9. Older generations are sometimes unwilling to accept new technologies, but _____ (driver) cars promise real value to these age groups, especially those having difficulty driving on their own.
10. In virtual classrooms the students can propose _____ (solve) to the assignments online.

Task 4 Rewrite the following sentences according to the examples.

Example 1: Autonomous learning can be referred to as student-centered learning *because it shifts the focus of education from teaching to learning.*
→Autonomous learning can be referred to as student-centered learning, *shifting the focus of education from teaching to learning.*

1. Sam told everything to Joan because he trusted her to keep secret.

2. John laughed into tears when he heard the news that he won the first prize.

3. As I know little about Russian culture, I make up my mind to study it from now on.

4. Because Europe produces less food than its people need, it must bring some products from other lands.

5. The doctor did not explain to the patient about the seriousness of his illness because he didn't want to make him nervous.

Example 2: It will help you schedule your study sessions to make sure you *have so much time that you can complete all your assignments.*
→It will help you schedule your study sessions to make sure you *have enough time to complete all your assignments.*

1. In my opinion, he is too young to take care of himself.

2. We were told that the river was so deep that we could swim in it.

3. As a child, he thought he had so much money that he could afford a plane.

4. I don't think we have so much power that we can take such a big order.

5. Years of college life have given me so much time that I have thought a lot about my future goals.

Task 5 — Complete the following English sentences using the words or phrases given in the brackets.

1. Many of the youngsters know the job in theory but _____ (当说到付诸实践), it _____ (还留有很多学习的空间). (when it comes to, leave room for)

2. Some teachers advise the students _____ (培养更好的学习习惯) and _____ (每天为课外活动留出一些时间). (study habits, set aside, extracurricular activities)

3. The student interacts with _____ (一台人工智能电脑而非真实的老师) who is to guide him through the lesson _____ (在虚拟世界里). (artificially intelligent, instead of, virtual world)

4. _____ (根据调查), the students with a growth mind-set felt _____ (达成学习目标更为重要) than to get good grades. (base on, it's important to, meet the goal)

5. In preparation for the test _____ (应该提供错误分析) to help the student _____ (从做习题中获得最大收益). (error analysis; get the most out of)

Applied writing

时间安排表

时间安排表是管理时间的一种方式。它是将某一时间段中已经明确的工作任务清晰地记载和表明的表格，是提醒使用人和相关人按照时间表的进程行动，有效管理时间、保证完成任务的简单方法。阅读下面的样例，了解时间安排表的特点。

Sample

A college student's daily timetable

Time	Content
6:30	Get up
7:00	Breakfast
7:30	Morning reading
8:00	The first class
8:50	The second class
9:30	Setting-up exercises during the break
10:00	The third class
10:50	The fourth class
11:30	Lunch
12:00	Midday rest
13:00	The fifth class
13:50	The sixth class
14:30	Eye exercises
15:00	The seventh class
15:50	The eighth class
16:30	Go home

Writing task

In order to balance study and entertainment wisely, Li Ming has listed his daily activities for himself. You are required to help make an English timetable for him according to the Chinese information given below.

- 7:30   起床
- 7:40   营养早餐
- 8:30   上课
- 9:55   课间休息（多多走动，开阔视野，避免近视，可提高下节课的效率）
- 11:40 午餐
- 12:20 午休
- 14:00 上课
- 17:30 晚餐
- 18:30 锻炼身体
- 20:00 图书馆晚修
- 23:00 上床睡觉

Words for reference

midday rest 午休

Project performing

💬 Guidelines

This project aims to simulate relevant situations of developing autonomous learning ability. The whole task is divided into three steps. Step one is about trying to figure out the importance of autonomous learning. Step two focuses on the effectiveness of time management skills. Step three is concerned with how to make a proper daily timetable.

Please follow the task description to complete the project.

Task description

Step one
- Organize a small group of 4 to 6 students in your class;
- Brainstorm and share the importance of autonomous learning;
- Give a presentation to air your views.

Step two
- List as many ways as possible that you manage your time;
- Divide the group into two sides: One side is for teacher-led learning, and the other side is for autonomous learning;
- Take turns to play roles: The first side asks questions on how to manage time effectively, and the other side gives answers.

Step three
- The side for teacher-led learning wants to know some time management skills, and the other side recommends making daily timetable with an example;
- Discuss what items to consider when making a practical daily timetable;
- Give a presentation to the whole class about your timetable.

Grammar

形容词和副词的原级、比较级和最高级

1. 比较级和最高级的变化形式

类别	原级	比较级	最高级
单音节单词，在后面加-er和-est	clean	cleaner	cleanest
重读闭音节单词，双写结尾的辅音字母，再加-er和-est	big sad	bigger sadder	biggest saddest
以e结尾的单词，在后面加-r和-st	nice large	nicer larger	nicest largest
以"辅音字母+y"结尾的单词，把y改成i，再加-er和-est	busy heavy	busier heavier	busiest heaviest
多音节单词，在前面加more和most	careful comfortable	more careful more comfortable	most careful most comfortable
不规则的变化形式	good/well bad/ill far much/many little	better worse farther/further more less	best worst farthest/furthest most least

2. 原级、比较级和最高级的特殊用法

特殊用法	例句
"the+形容词原级" 指一类人或物，在句中做主语时，谓语动词用复数形式	*The old* are more likely to catch cold than the young. *The sick* were allowed to pass free.
原级比较： (1) 肯定句：as+原级+as（像……一样） (2) 否定句：not so/as+原级+ as…	Art is *as interesting as* music. English is *not so difficult as* science.
比较级前的修饰语常用 much, far, even, a lot, a little, rather, somewhat 等	It's *much colder* than it was yesterday. Houses are *far more expensive* these days.
and 连接两个比较级表示程度加深，意为 "越来越……"	Computers are becoming *more and more* complicated. Old Johnson grew *fatter and fatter*.
"the+比较级…, the+比较级…" 意为 "越……越……"	*The more* money you make, *the more* you spend. *The more* expensive petrol becomes, *the less* people drive.
三者或三者以上比较： the+最高级+of/in/among…（副词最高级前的the可省略）	Spring is *the best* season *of* the year. He jumped *(the) farthest of* all.
times 表示三倍以上比较： (1) …times+as+原级+as… (2) …times the size (height/length/width) of…	Asia is *four times as large as* Europe. The new building is *four times the size of* the old one.

Task 1 Choose the best answer to complete each of the following sentences.

1. Mike looks _____ than Paul, but they are of the same age.
   A. youngest B. the youngest C. younger D. very young
2. Beijing is the capital of China and it is _____ bigger than many other cities in China.
   A. little B. few C. some D. much
3. —Who's _____ basketball player in China now? Is it Yao Ming?
   —No. It's Sun Mingming.
   A. tall B. taller C. the tallest D. the taller
4. The more regularly we eat, the _____ we are.
   A. healthy B. healthier C. healthiest D. health
5. When spring comes, it gets _____.
   A. warm and warm B. colder and colder C. warmer and warmer D. shorter and shorter
6. Listening is just as _____ as speaking in language learning.
   A. important B. more important C. most important D. the most important

7. Lucy didn't make any mistakes in the math exam. She is _____ than any other students in the class.

   A. the most careful　　　　　　　　B. more careless

   C. more careful　　　　　　　　　　D. much careful

8. Mrs. Black has got _____ instead of getting any better.

   A. more bad　　　　　　　　　　　B. a little worse

   C. much badly　　　　　　　　　　D. a lot of worse

9. The earth is about _____ as the moon.

   A. as fifty time big　　　　　　　　B. fifty times as big

   C. as big fifty times　　　　　　　　D. fifty is times big

10. All of us want to do more work with _____ time and _____ workers.

    A. fewer; less　　　　　　　　　　B. less; fewer

    C. more; much　　　　　　　　　　D. less; more

Task 2 Complete the following sentences with the proper forms of the given adjectives or adverbs.

1. James played as _____ as you. Mary played _____ _____ of all. (well)
2. A dictionary is much _____ (expensive) than a story book.
3. I drove ten miles _____ (far) than necessary.
4. I bought the _____ (late) edition of today's paper.
5. It's a favorite resort for the _____ (rich).
6. The rain cleared _____ (quickly) than I expected.
7. Sylvia sings as _____ (sweetly) as her sister.
8. Taking taxi is the _____ (easy) way to get to the airport.
9. The more he eats, the _____ (fat) he gets.
10. My sister is three kilos _____ (heavy) than I.

Task 3 Translate the following sentences into English.

1. 我打字越快，出的错越多。
2. 我在有压力时干活最快。
3. 这是这个国家最糟糕的一段公路。
4. 她不能像比利跳得那么高。
5. 据说英国人有一种特殊的幽默感。

Self-evaluation

Rate your own progress in this unit.	D	M	P	F*
I can say words about study plan in English.	☐	☐	☐	☐
I can tell the importance of autonomous learning.	☐	☐	☐	☐
I can manage my time more effectively.	☐	☐	☐	☐
I can make my study plan by myself.	☐	☐	☐	☐
I can make my daily timetable in English.	☐	☐	☐	☐
I can master usages of adjectives and adverbs.	☐	☐	☐	☐

*Note: D (Distinction), M (Merit), P (Pass), F (Fail)

Culture

进入大学后,我们的时间不再有老师帮忙打理。于是,忽然间我们有了大把的时间,却不知如何好好地管理。似乎一天从早忙到晚,可并未完成任何事情。这是为什么呢?

因为我们忘记除了为自己的学业制订目标外,还应该制订一套科学可行的学习计划来实现这个目标!

制订学习计划的作用
- 计划是实现目标的蓝图
- 促使自己实施计划
- 有利于养成良好的学习习惯
- 合理的计划安排能够更有效地利用时间

怎么制订学习计划
- 计划要考虑全面
- 长远计划和短期安排
- 安排好常规学习时间和自由学习时间
- 突出学习重点
- 从实际出发制订计划

Unit 2 | Autonomous Learning 53

 Task 1 Watch the following video clip, and then complete the table with missing words and phrases.

Making a study schedule

A study schedule is nothing more than a tool of your ___1___. You need one to help you remain focused on the things that are important and to keep yourself ___2___. So here are the six steps to a successful study schedule.	1. Place your fixed commitments into the schedule.
	2. Create a realistic schedule.
	  Some people create a schedule with every moment of their day ___3___. That does work for some students, but it doesn't work for most.
	3. Create achievable goals.
	  Don't write down things like getting the highest grade in each of your classes or getting the best grade on a test. That is outside of your control.
	4. Write down the steps for each goal.
	  It is the steps that you will place into your schedule.
	5. Remain flexible.
	  Life will ___4___ you. Just don't get frustrated, and realize that moving things around is normal.
	6. Make time for yourself.
	  Include time for breaks, exercises, cooking, laundry, entertainment.
	  Once you create a plan and you've used it for a week, spend a few minutes at the end of the week ___5___ it. See what worked and what didn't work. Again this is your tool, so make sure it's working for you.

Task 2 Make up a weekly study schedule of yourself.

Unit 3
On-campus Training

Learning objectives

After studying this unit, you should be able to:
- get familiar with the words and expressions concerning campus training;
- know more about campus training and its benefits;
- have some idea of campus jobs;
- be clear about how to prepare for a career in a specific field;
- master the skills of writing a campus training report;
- be expert at the usages of simple tenses.

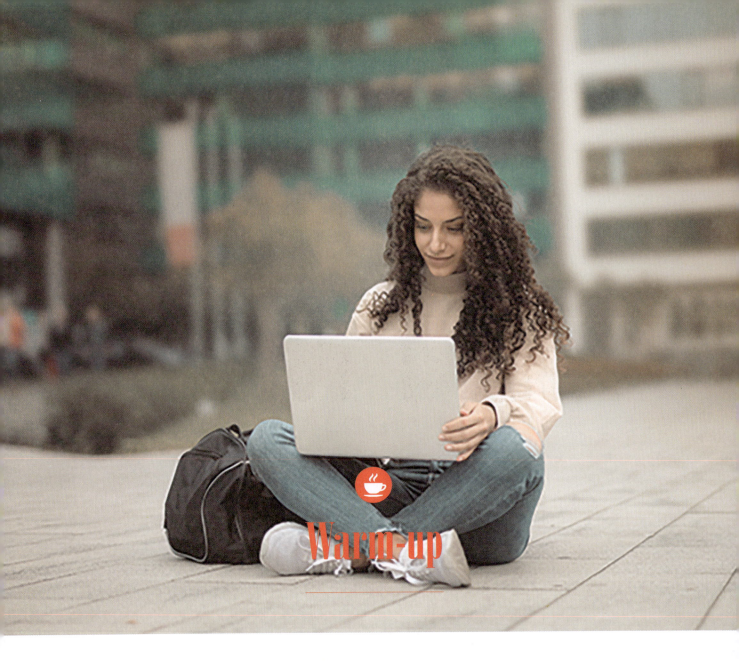

Task 1 Look at the following two pictures and answer the questions.

Pic. 1

Pic. 2

1. What learning methods are mentioned in Picture 1? How useful is each method?
2. How does Xun Zi compare these methods in Picture 2?
3. What is the best learning method according to these two pictures?

Task 2 Look at the following pictures and answer the questions.

"I work as a Student Ambassador on campus. It's an amazingly varied role, ranging from helping year 6 students to program Lego robots one day, to touring a group of 20 prospective students and their parents the next. I enjoy meeting so many different people—it's a great buzz! I've gained a great deal of experience from my role, including leadership, management and teamwork. Head to Campus Jobs and get applying."

Notes

Student Ambassador	/æmˈbæsədə/		学生大使
Lego robots			乐高机器人
prospective	/prəˈspektɪv/	a.	预期的；潜在的

1. What is the campus job shown in the above pictures?
2. What did Jack Abrey do when he worked as a Student Ambassador?
3. What has Jack Abrey gained from his campus job?
4. Can you name some other campus jobs?

Reading A

In a badminton match, Li Ming and a junior student, Chen Ling, become good friends. Chen Ling is from School of Finance and Trade. One day they study together in the library and Li Ming notices "On-campus training" in Chen Ling's class schedule. Li Ming feels very curious so he asks Chen Ling for more about it. Chen Ling shares with him what she knows and recommends him an article *Campus training program* as below.

> **Pre-reading questions**
> 1. What is campus training?
> 2. What benefits can students get from campus training programs?

Campus training program

Campus training, as its name implies, refers to training that is given on the campus. It is also called on-campus training. This kind of training is not ordinary as it contains all the important aspects, which are essential for students to know before entering into the expert world. Generally speaking, campus training programs can provide students with professional trainers, and latest methodologies of learning, and attach more importance to practical learning than to theoretical learning. These factors will surely make a vital difference in shaping up the career of a student.

These training programs provide opportunities for students to apply knowledge to practical work. For some programs, the training hours are flexible, and students can arrange their own training schedules to fit their class timetable. In this case, students can utilize their spare time to gain actual work experiences through on-the-job training provided by the school authority as well as the participation in school activities. Through the training period, they would assist in administrative work, frontline services, computer room management, organizing activities, designing promotion materials, etc.

For other programs, experts from industries or companies will stay in college to conduct the training. They usually prefer 5 to 6 hours a day and a one-week schedule. Of course, the final schedule is usually worked out with the school authority in order to be convenient to all. The programs are specially outlined by the experts according to the appeal of industries so that they can prepare students in line with the present need in order to boost their placement prospect. Placement training will also be conducted in the college premises, which includes technical and soft skills training. In view of the fact that college students can be better guided by youngsters, a group of young engineers from the industry are often invited to serve as trainers who will keep the students motivated and attentive throughout the sessions.

Campus training programs also aim at enhancing students' personal development. Through different events like team building training, outbound trip, tea meeting, practical workshop, etc., students can enrich their social circle and strengthen their team spirit. To recognize trainees' hard work for the year, some universities would hold the Award Ceremony annually. Outstanding trainees will even be subsidized to the summer exchange program.

Campus training programs are especially beneficial to students. Time of students is saved because they do not have to go out for getting trained. Money of students is also saved because on-campus training programs are free of charge in most cases, or much cheaper than off-campus training programs. What's more, training within the campus can build up students' confidence, and facilitate the development of a sense of belonging to the university and to the society. And most importantly, such experiences can enhance students' personal competitiveness in the future job market.

(467 words)

New words

*imply	/ɪmˈplaɪ/	v.	意味；暗示
*contain	/kənˈteɪn/	v.	包含；含有
*essential	/ɪˈsenʃl/	a.	基本的；必要的
▲methodology	/ˌmeθəˈdɒlədʒi/	n.	方法学，方法论
*attach	/əˈtætʃ/	v.	贴上；系上
▲theoretical	/ˌθɪəˈretɪkl/	a.	理论的；理论上的
*vital	/ˈvaɪtl/	a.	至关重要的
*flexible	/ˈfleksəbl/	a.	灵活的；柔韧的
*utilize	/ˈjuːtəlaɪz/	v.	利用
*authority	/ɔːˈθɒrəti/	n.	当局；权威
▲participation	/pɑːˌtɪsɪˈpeɪʃn/	n.	参与
▲youngster	/ˈjʌŋstə(r)/	n.	年轻人；少年
*outline	/ˈaʊtlaɪn/	v.	概述；显示……的轮廓
*appeal	/əˈpiːl/	n.	吸引力，魅力
▲boost	/buːst/	v.	使增长；提升
▲placement	/ˈpleɪsmənt/	n.	就业；(对人的)安置，安排
*prospect	/ˈprɒspekt/	n.	可能性；希望；前景
▲premise	/ˈpremɪs/	n.	办公场所
*motivate	/ˈməʊtɪveɪt/	v.	激励；成为……的动机
▲attentive	/əˈtentɪv/	a.	留心的，注意的
*enhance	/ɪnˈhɑːns/	v.	提高；加强

outbound	/ˈaʊtbaʊnd/	a.	出境的；向外去的
▲subsidize	/ˈsʌbsɪdaɪz/	v.	资助；给予奖助金
*beneficial	/ˌbenɪˈfɪʃl/	a.	有益的，有利的
▲facilitate	/fəˈsɪlɪteɪt/	v.	促进；帮助
competitiveness	/kəmˈpetətɪvnəs/	n.	竞争（力）

Phrases & expressions

attach importance to	重视
shape up	形成
apply… to…	把……应用于
work out	制订出
in line with	与……一致
in view of	鉴于
on-campus training	校内实训
practical learning	实践学习
theoretical learning	理论学习
on-the-job training	岗位培训；在职培训
administrative work	行政工作
frontline service	一线服务
placement training	就业培训
team building	团队建设
summer exchange program	暑期交换生项目

生词数	生词率	*B级词汇	*A级词汇	▲四、六级词汇	超纲词汇
27	5.78%	9	6	10	2

Notes

1. on/off-campus training program

The on-campus training program is organized in a college or university and accommodates many of the real facets. It is considered as compulsory because it holds all the attributes that prepare students for the corporate world and makes them understand the practical elements of a particular area. Whereas, the off-campus training involves the migration of students to a professional workplace where practical perception is delivered on a major level than the theoretical knowledge.

2. campus placement

Campus placement is a program conducted within universities or other educational institutions to provide jobs to students nearing completion of their studies. In this type of program, the educational institutions partner with corporations who wish to recruit from the student population.

3. on-the-job training

On-the-job training is a form of training provided at the workplace. During the training, employees are familiarized with the working environment they will become part of. Employees also get a hands-on experience using machinery, equipment, tools, materials, etc. Part of on-the-job training is to face the challenges that occur during the performance of the job. An experienced employee or a manager is executing the role of the mentor who is passing on his/her knowledge and company-specific skills to the new employees through written or verbal instructions and demonstrations.

After-reading tasks

Task 1 Read the passage and fill in the blanks with appropriate information from the passage.

Campus training programs are conducted at college campus. These training programs provide opportunities for students to apply ___1___ to practical work. For some programs, the training hours are flexible, and students can arrange their own training schedules to fit their ___2___. Students can use their spare time to gain actual ___3___ by participating in school activities. For other programs, ___4___ from industries will stay in college to conduct the training. The programs are specially outlined by the experts so that they can prepare students in line with the present need in order to boost their placement ___5___.

Task 2 Read the passage again and decide whether the following statements are true (T) or false (F). If it is false, write the key words to support your answer.

(   ) 1. Campus training programs provide opportunities for students to apply knowledge to practical work.

(   ) 2. For some programs, experts from industries will stay in college to conduct the training but the schedule should be mainly convenient to the experts.

(   ) 3. A group of young engineers from the industry are often invited to serve as trainers because they can keep the students motivated and attentive.

(   ) 4. Money of students is saved because on-campus training programs are free of charge in all cases.

(   ) 5. Outstanding trainees will even be subsidized to the summer exchange program.

Listening and speaking

Task 1 The article *Campus training program* really opens a new world to Li Ming. He never imagines that students can get jobs on campus. He feels very excited and talks over this with his father on the phone. His father totally agrees that Li Ming should apply for one and shares his opinions on campus jobs. Listen to his remarks three times and complete the following note.

Campus jobs provide a useful	• _____ for college students.
Campus jobs are your gateway to different	• _____ jobs at the college.
You could be working one week in one campus	• _____ or _____.
The other week you could do a research	• _____ in your department.
Campus jobs give the opportunity to	• _____ some money.
Campus jobs provide necessary	• _____ experience in a trusted environment.
With campus jobs, you can make valuable	• _____ and develop your employment skills.
Campus jobs give you a great	• _____ when looking for a _____ job.

Unit 3 | On-campus Training

Task 2 With the encouragement from his father, Li Ming decides to apply for one campus job, but he has no idea about where to start, so he turns to Chen Ling for help. Listen to their conversation three times and choose the best answers to complete the following sentences.

1. This conversation most probably takes place _____.
   A. in the computer lab   B. in a classroom   C. on the playground   D. in the dormitory
2. To get an on-campus job, Li Ming needs to prepare _____ at first.
   A. a CV   B. network   C. people skills   D. employment skills
3. The easiest way to get an on-campus job is to ask your _____.
   A. classmates   B. juniors   C. seniors   D. parents
4. Another common way to apply for an on-campus job is to go to _____.
   A. student union   B. Career Services Center   C. library   D. placement center
5. A very creative way to get an on-campus job is to join _____.
   A. computer lab   B. Career Services Center   C. library   D. student organizations

Task 3 In addition to campus jobs, campus training can be on-the-job training programs guided by the experts from industries or companies, who work out the program schedules together with the school authority. Li Ming wonders what campus training he may have for his own major, so he talks to Mrs. Song and asks her to explain the details to him. Listen to their conversation three times and fill in the blanks.

Li Ming: Mrs. Song, could you please tell me what campus training programs are scheduled for my major?

Mrs. Song: Well, one of the programs is operational budgets. It is a two-week training program guided by the experts from one company. You need to ___1___ and record operational budgets for ___2___ companies.

Li Ming: Is it difficult? If I ___3___ this program successfully, what can I learn from it?

Mrs. Song: Not easy. By the end of the program, you will be able to prepare the budget, set the budget time ___4___, manage the follow-up and record the budget. You need to be very patient and careful when doing all of these.

Li Ming: And what do I need to hand in?

Mrs. Song: A lot of ___5___. They need to be filled in based on the information provided.

Li Ming: Wow, I have to face a lot of ___6___ and calculation. That's really a ___7___ for me.

Mrs. Song: That's why you need more ___8___. You will feel better if you can exercise and ___9___ again and again. All the calculations are to be completed by hand. If you can make sure to record the financial information ___10___ in every table, you will be a good employee in future.

Li Ming: Thanks a lot, professor, I will try my best.

Task 4 On the day when Chen Ling is scheduled to attend her campus training, Li Ming calls her to ask if she could go together to experience the campus training with him. Chen Ling is happy to have his company and they decide to meet and walk to the training room together. On their way, they continue to talk about campus training. Listen to their conversation three times and tick off the items mentioned.

☐ 1. improve personal development ☐ 2. limit personal development
☐ 3. soft skills ☐ 4. enrich our social circle
☐ 5. strengthen our team spirit ☐ 6. technical skills
☐ 7. increase the gap ☐ 8. bridge the gap
☐ 9. increase the income ☐ 10. build up our confidence

Task 5 Suppose you are Li Ming and your partner is the expert from a company to guide you with the hands-on training. You turn to him to ask for the detailed instruction for the training. Make up a dialogue and role-play it in class.

Task 6 The following are four benefits concerning campus training. Discuss them with your partner, and then tell each other which one you care most and why.

- Campus training provides chances to earn some money.
- Campus training can enrich our social circle.
- Campus training can help shape up our future career.
- Campus training provides us more with hands-on learning and application.

Reading B

After the finance training ends, Li Ming has enough time to read carefully the training manual Chen Ling sent him by WeChat. Below is the manual *Campus training programs to prepare students for life in finance*.

Campus training programs to prepare students for life in finance

To bridge the gap between academics and the real world, we work with career centers, student clubs and professors to prepare college students for a career in finance. Our experienced instructors, all former investment bankers, will teach the practical application of topics most trainees have only seen on a theoretical level. We can offer different kinds of programs as follows:

1-weekend financial & valuation modeling boot camp

This is a live training program. It prepares students for interviews and the job by equipping them with a real-world financial and valuation modeling skill set. We work with all group sizes to deliver the core analyst skill set of financial and valuation modeling with a focus on Excel best practices and efficiency.

Wall Street passport

This is an all-in-one online training program. It picks up where the academic textbook leaves off to teach students the real-world Excel, financial analysis and Powerpoint skills bankers use most before taking them step by step through the financial and valuation model-building process. This program gives them the opportunity to take a deeper dive into advanced modeling and shows them how to display these skills during recruitment.

2-weekend financial & valuation modeling boot camp

This is a live training program. It exposes students to the core financial modeling skill set of investment banking analysts and associates. Designed for students pursuing careers in finance and investment banking in particular, this program will prepare students for both finance interviews and the demands of an analyst or associate position.

1-weekend financial modeling boot camp for liberal arts students

This is a live training program. Liberal arts students face an uphill battle during the finance recruiting process. We offer a version of its popular on-campus financial modeling boot camp that's designed specifically for liberal arts majors who have had limited exposure to accounting, finance and Excel. The goal of the program is to prepare liberal arts students with the real-world financial and valuation modeling skill set they need to succeed in interviews and on the job.

1-2 day technical finance interview preparation

This is a live training program. It shows students headed into recruitment how to effectively answer common finance interview questions. We begin with an overview of the financial industry. Students then progress step by step through accounting, valuation, M&A and leveraged buyout concepts commonly encountered in the technical interview. We pay particular attention to the level of detail needed to construct comprehensive answers that won't leave interviewees vulnerable to increasingly technical follow-ups. By the end of the program, students will understand how to articulate key finance and accounting concepts in concise and well-structured responses.

(450 words)

New words

*gap	/gæp/	n.	缺口；间隔；差距
*academic	/ˌækəˈdemɪk/	n.	学术知识
▲finance	/ˈfaɪnæns/	n.	财政；金融
*former	/ˈfɔːmə(r)/	a.	前者的；前任的
valuation	/ˌvæljuˈeɪʃn/	n.	评价，估价
*live	/laɪv/	a.	实况转播的，现场表演的
*financial	/faɪˈnænʃl/	a.	金融的；财务的
▲deliver	/dɪˈlɪvə(r)/	vt.	交付；发表
▲analyst	/ˈænəlɪst/	n.	分析者
▲efficiency	/ɪˈfɪʃnsi/	n.	效能；功效
▲display	/dɪˈspleɪ/	vt.	展示；显露，表现
▲recruitment	/rɪˈkruːtmənt/	n.	招收，招聘

▲expose	/ɪkˈspəʊz/	vt.	使曝光，使暴露
▲core	/kɔː(r)/	n.	核心；要点
▲associate	/əˈsəʊsieɪt/	n.	同事；伙伴；合伙人
		a.	有关联的
uphill	/ˌʌpˈhɪl/	a.	上坡的；向上的
*version	/ˈvɜːʃn/	n.	版本
▲exposure	/ɪkˈspəʊzə(r)/	n.	暴露；曝光
overview	/ˈəʊvəvjuː/	n.	概述；纵览；概论
▲encounter	/ɪnˈkaʊntə(r)/	v.	遭遇；邂逅
▲comprehensive	/ˌkɒmprɪˈhensɪv/	a.	详尽的；综合性的
▲vulnerable	/ˈvʌlnərəbl/	a.	易受攻击的，易受伤害的
▲articulate	/ɑːˈtɪkjuleɪt/	vt.	明确表达；清楚说明
follow-up	/ˈfɒləʊ ʌp/	n.	后续行动；后续事物
		a.	后继的；跟进的
▲concise	/kənˈsaɪs/	a.	简明的；简洁的

💬 Phrases & expressions

bridge the gap	缩小差距
pick up	拾起；捡起
leave off	停止；中断
succeed in (doing) sth.	在……上取得成功
step by step	一步一步地；逐步地
career center	就业中心
student club	学生俱乐部
investment banker	投资银行家
financial & valuation modeling boot camp	财务与估值建模新兵训练营
financial and valuation modeling skill set	财务与估值建模技能
financial industry	金融业
M&A	(=merge and acquisition)并购，兼并与收购
leveraged buyout	融资收购；融资买入
technical follow-ups	技术跟进

生词数	生词率	*B级词汇	*A级词汇	▲四、六级词汇	超纲词汇
26	5.58%	3	3	16	4

After-reading tasks

Task 1 Complete the following table with information taken from the passage.

Program	Goal
1-weekend financial & valuation modeling boot camp	prepares students for ___1___ and the job by equipping them with a real-world financial and valuation modeling skill set.
Wall Street passport	teaches students the real-world Excel, ___2___ and PowerPoint skills.
2-weekend financial & valuation modeling boot camp	prepares students for both finance interviews and ___3___ of an analyst or associate position.
1-weekend financial modeling boot camp for liberal arts students	prepares ___4___ with the real-world financial and valuation modeling skill set.
1-2 day technical finance interview preparation	helps students understand how to ___5___ key finance and accounting concepts.

Task 2 Translate the following paragraph into Chinese.

This is an all-in-one online training program. It picks up where the academic textbook leaves off to teach students the real-world Excel, financial analysis and PowerPoint skills bankers use most before taking them step by step through the financial and valuation model-building process. This program gives them the opportunity to take a deeper dive into advanced modeling and shows them how to display these skills during recruitment.

Unit 3 | On-campus Training

Comprehensive exercises

Task 1 Fill in the blanks with the words or expressions from Readings A and B according to the meanings in the right column. The first letter of each word is already given to help your spelling. Then compare your answers with your partner.

f_____	able to change to suit new conditions or situations
u_____	to use something, especially for a practical purpose
b_____	to make something increase, or become better or more successful
s_____	to pay part of the cost of something
f_____	to make something easier or more likely to happen
m_____	to cause someone to behave in a particular way; to make someone eager to do something
e_____	to give someone the skills needed to do a particular thing
s_____	to start to develop or to seem likely to happen
p_____	to lift up
l_____	to stop, or to stop doing something

Task 2 Complete the following sentences with the words and expressions from Task 1. Change the form if necessary.

1. We should learn to grasp communication skills for they can _____ understanding between different people.
2. I'm fortunate because my job has _____ hours, and I can come and go pretty much as I want.
3. A basic two-hour first aid course would _____ you to deal with any of these incidents.
4. During that period of hard times, the theatre managed to _____ its audiences by cutting ticket prices.
5. Little Jack quickly _____ the keys from the playground and handed them over to his class-master.
6. Once Tom starts doing something, he won't _____ until he's finished it.
7. Though only 14 years old, John is almost 1.8 meters in height. We all believe that he will _____ into an excellent basketball player.
8. He says that to _____ the operation, around two-thirds of the older buildings would be rented out for shops and restaurants.
9. It is said that Chinese were the first to _____ sharp stones as hunting tools in old times.
10. Your advertisement must attract consumers' attention, create a desire for your product, and _____ people to take action to buy it.

Task 3 Complete the following sentences with the appropriate forms of the words given in the brackets.

1. To be honest, I'm not very _____ (practice), and I can't even change a light bulb.
2. We should develop students' abilities to _____ (application) theory to practice.
3. With all the programs, teamwork is key as _____ (train) learn the importance of leadership and being part of a bigger task.
4. We do wish the government would be more _____ (attention) to the problem of air pollution.
5. Believe it or not, it is very important to learn how to display your skills during _____ (recruit).
6. Early findings suggest that a bigger breakfast is _____ (benefit) to weight control.
7. Education is seen as a way to ensure economic _____ (compete) and continued economic growth.
8. They were laughing loudly, without noticing the fact that they were on a _____ (life) TV show.
9. Their company's _____ (finance) position is not certain because their products can't meet the needs of customers.
10. Advertisements featuring professional sportsmen and their supported products tend to get impressive _____ (expose) on TV, radio, in print and online.

Task 4 Rewrite the following sentences according to the examples.

Example 1: A group of young engineers from the industry are often invited to serve as trainers *who will keep the students motivated and attentive* throughout the sessions.
→ A group of young engineers from the industry are often invited to serve as trainers *to keep the students motivated and attentive* throughout the sessions.

1. She offered me a cup of coffee which will refresh my spirit.

2. I work with Jackie who is a pleasant fellow.

3. Are you going to the conference which will be held next week?

4. Do I have your promise that you won't tell anyone about this?

5. Many students have such an expectation that they can take more reviewing classes before the final exam.

Example 2: They usually prefer 5 to 6 hours a day and *a schedule that lasts for one week*.
→ They usually prefer 5 to 6 hours a day and <u>*a one-week schedule*</u>.

1. It is clear that most college students prefer training that is given on the campus.
   _____

2. We haven't thought that the famous writer is a young man who is only 23 years old.
   _____

3. If you want to become a QC engineer in this company, you can apply to get training that is given on the spot.
   _____

4. Mrs. Johnson told us that her big family used to live in an old building that had two stories.
   _____

5. It was not surprising that they refused to buy that table that only had three legs even at a very lower price.
   _____

Task 5 Complete the following English sentences using the words or phrases given in the brackets.

1. We should _____ (更加重视) developing students' ability to _____ (把知识运用到实际工作中去). (attach importance to, apply… to)

2. The manager asked his assistant if it is possible to _____ (制订一个营销计划) _____ (符合) their tight budget. (work out, in line with)

3. A happy smile can _____ (架起陌生人之间的桥梁) even if language barriers prevent them from _____ (表达自己的情感). (bridge a gap between, articulate)

4. The plan aims at _____ (促进员工的个人发展) and _____ (激励他们走向更美好的未来). (enhance, motivate, head)

5. For better performance at work new employees will _____ (接受岗位培训) to _____ (强化技术和通用技能). (on-the-job training, technical and soft skills)

Applied writing

实训报告

实训报告是个人在学习某一技能的过程中，通过动手实践、观察、分析、综合、判断，如实记录实训的全部过程和实训结果的书面材料，内容包含实训目的、实训环境、实训原理、实训过程、实训结果、实训总结等方面的内容。实训报告具有情报交流的作用和保留资料的作用。阅读下面的样例，了解实训报告的特点。

Sample

A campus training report from a student majoring in accounting

Information about the training

Training program:	Practice of bank teller
Place:	Computer room (Room 1432)
Date:	May 10 to 16, 2021 (one-week training)
Trainer:	Professor Lin

To bridge the gap between academics and the real world, we took part in a one-week training program as a bank teller to prepare ourselves for a career in accounting in computer room (Room 1432) from May 10 to May 16, 2021.

During the training period, we learned the techniques to count cash quickly, and the workflow as well. We also learned about how to fill in different kinds of forms and receipts concerning accounting.

From this campus training program, I got a new experience and realized that it is important to work diligently and carefully in the real banking world.

Writing task

Li Ming has strong interest in selling things and he plans to find a part-time job as a salesperson. So he attends a three-day on-campus training program on sales. You are required to help him with his training report according to the Chinese information given below.

培训项目：销售培训
培训日期：2022年6月26日至28日
培训内容：
　第一天　户外培训：团队建设
　第二、三天　室内培训：公司文化、公司产品、产品推销要点、销售技巧、人际关系技巧、自我激励等
　特邀演讲嘉宾：推销训练大师 Mr. Kang

Words for reference

1. 特邀演讲嘉宾 guest speaker
2. 自我激励 self-encouragement/self-motivation
3. 团队建设 team building
4. 推销训练大师 sales trainer

Project performing

💬 Guidelines

This project aims to simulate relevant situations of conducting on-campus training. The whole task is divided into three steps. Step one is about trying to find out the importance of on-campus training. Step two focuses on actual conducting of on-campus training. Step three is concerned with writing a campus training report.

Please follow the task description to complete the project.

Task description

Step one
- Organize a small group of 4 to 6 students in your class;
- Brainstorm and share the importance of on-campus training;
- Give a presentation to introduce the effect of on-campus training on future career.

Step two
- List as many campus training programs as possible that your school can offer to students;
- Divide the group into two sides: One side is trainers, the other is trainees;
- Take turns to play roles: The side of trainers demonstrates how to train learners effectively, and the other side follows them carefully.

Step three
- The side of trainers asks for opinions about a certain program, and the side of trainees writes a training report accordingly;
- Discuss the training report with group members;
- Give a presentation to the whole class about your training report.

一般时态的基本用法和特殊用法

1. 一般现在时

基本用法/特殊用法	例句
表示经常发生或反复发生的动作，现在的情况或状态，永恒的真理	She works eight hours a day. They live in the same building. The sun rises in the east.
在口语中可表示按规定、计划或时间表将要发生的事情，后接表示未来时间的状语	The plane takes off at 9:20 a.m. Those players arrive here tomorrow afternoon.
在时间或条件状语从句中，用一般现在时表示将来的动作	I'll discuss this with you when we meet. I won't write unless he writes first.
报纸标题中常用一般现在时谈论最近发生的事件	FIRE BREAKS OUT IN HOTEL ROOM FOREIGN MINISTER RESIGNS

2. 一般将来时

基本用法/特殊用法	例句
表示将要发生的事情，常用"will+动词原形"；shall常用于第一人称	We will know the result tomorrow. Where shall we go for holiday?
表示提出请求	Will you please be quiet?
be going to 结构表示打算做某事或即将发生某事	He is going to buy her some flowers. It's going to rain soon.
be+不定式结构可表示将要发生的动作或已经安排好的事情	She is to be married next month. The expedition is to start in a week's time.
be about to 结构表示就要发生的事情	Turn off the gas. The soup is about to boil over. Quick, jump in! The train is about to leave.

3. 一般过去时

基本用法/特殊用法	例句
表示过去发生的动作或存在的状态	I got to know her in 2008. She suffered a lot in her childhood.
在口语中，一般过去时可代替一般现在时，使语气更客气和委婉	I wondered if you could do me a favor. I hoped you could give me some advice.
与一般过去时连用的时间状语需指过去的时间，如 yesterday, last summer, …ago等	I met Robert many years ago. George came in just now.

Task 1 Complete the following sentences using proper forms of the given verbs.

1. Mike sometimes _____ (go) to park with his sister.
2. The concert _____ (begin) at 7:30 next Friday evening.
3. If I _____ (see) Nancy, I'll ask her.
4. QUAKE _____ (hit) CENTRAL IRAN (News Headline)
5. It _____ (be) warm tomorrow.
6. When she _____ (come), I'll tell her about it.
7. The Prime Minister _____ (visit) Hungary in May.
8. —When did this happen?
   —It _____ (happen) in the Han Dynasty.
9. I _____ (wonder) if you could give me a lift.
10. She _____ (be) here a minute ago.

Task 2 Choose the best answer to complete each of the following sentences.

1. He said the sun _____ in the east and _____ in the west.
   A. rose; set   B. rises; sets   C. rises; set   D. rise; sets
2. On Sunday, he sometimes _____ his clothes and sometimes _____ some shopping.
   A. wash; do   B. washes; does   C. is washing; is doing   D. washed; did
3. _____ to Turkey every year for your holiday?
   A. Are you going   B. Were you going   C. Have you gone   D. Do you go
4. Kathy _____ back a few minutes ago.
   A. has come   B. comes   C. came   D. come
5. After she _____ hospital, she had a long holiday.
   A. leaves   B. is leaving   C. has left   D. left

6. If Jack _____ , I'll let you know.
   A. phones   B. is phoning
   C. phoned   D. has phoned

7. —Has anybody offered to look after the children?
   —Jo _____ it.
   A. is to do   B. does
   C. did   D. will do

8. When you _____ Dave, tell him he still owes me some money.
   A. are going to see   B. are seeing
   C. see   D. will see

9. In the next few years, thousands of speed cameras _____ on major roads.
   A. are appear   B. appear
   C. are to appear   D. are appearing

10. When I worked as a postman, I _____ up at 3 o'clock every morning.
    A. get   B. got
    C. is getting   D. has got

Task 3 Translate the following sentences into English.

1. 他们住在同一栋楼，对吧？
2. 万一我忘了，请提醒我。
3. 今晚我不打算和你争论。
4. 昨天我们两人开会都迟到了。
5. 天暖和一点雪就会开始融化。

Self-evaluation

Rate your own progress in this unit.	D	M	P	F*
I can say words and expressions about campus training in English.	☐	☐	☐	☐
I can tell the benefits of campus training.	☐	☐	☐	☐
I can know more about campus jobs and training.	☐	☐	☐	☐
I can prepare for a career in a specific field.	☐	☐	☐	☐
I can write a campus training report.	☐	☐	☐	☐
I can master the usages of simple tenses, simple future tense and simple past tense.	☐	☐	☐	☐

*Note: D (Distinction), M (Merit), P (Pass), F (Fail)

Culture

实训是指以职业为导向的实践型教学环节。实训教学采用来自真实工作项目的实际案例，教学过程中注重理论结合实践，更强调学生的参与式学习。实训教学能够在最短的时间内使学生在专业技能、实践经验、工作方法、团队合作等方面取得进步。

实训的最终目的是全面提高学生的职业素质，最终达到学生满意就业、企业满意用人的目的。从开展场所上分类，有校内实训和校外实训，包括教学见习、教学实训和生产实训。从形式上分类，有技能鉴定达标实训和岗位素质达标实训，包括通用技能实训和专项技能实训。从内容上分类，有动手操作技能实训和心智技能实训，包括综合素质要求实训。从程度上分类，有单项实训和综合实训。从结构上分类，有岗位训练、过程训练、项目/任务训练、仿真训练等模式。

Task 1 **Watch the following video clip, and then complete the passage with the words or phrases you hear.**

China improving technical and vocational education and training

For twenty-year-old Wei Binchang, learning the art of using survey equipment now takes place in ____1____ rather than in the classroom. Wei Binchang credits the change to recent reforms at his technical school in Guangzhou.

Every year in China, more than eleven million students like Wei Binchang enroll for technical or ____2____ training. A World Bank funded project is helping three technical schools in Guangdong Province meet these challenges. The goal is to better prepare students like Wu Di, who dreams of becoming a chemical analyst for today's ____3____ job market. The project also helps retrain instructors in modernized curricula.

A key focus is building up links between schools and industry. Industry experts are invited to teach, and joint labs help students directly take part in company ____4____. It's a partnership that's paying off. Students have the chance to test their skills, from interning in an optical shop to working as a flight attendant.

It's hoped the lessons learnt in Guangdong Province can be shared with other vocational schools across China. And so help the country ____5____ its skilled workforce.

Task 2 **List the curriculum of one hands-on training course of your major, and try to recognize the skills you can learn from it.**

Unit 4
Community Service

Learning objectives

After studying this unit, you should be able to:
- get familiar with the words and expressions concerning community service;
- understand the importance of community service;
- know more about community service and how to get involved in it;
- be clear about different types of community service;
- master the skills of writing a poster;
- be expert at the usages of continuous tenses.

Warm-up

Task 1 Watch the video and answer the following questions orally. Some key words and phrases are listed for you.

> legal consultancy 法律咨询　　left-behind children 留守儿童　　heartfelt thanks 衷心感谢
> dedication 奉献精神　　ever-expanding 不断发展的

1. What does volunteers' work aim to?
2. Who are teaming up to provide community service in Chengdu, Sichuan Province?
3. What community service activities are mentioned in the video?
4. What spirit does volunteers' work involve?

Task 2 Look at the following pictures and match each of them with the corresponding community service activity.

> **A.** rubbish collecting　　**B.** street cleaning　　**C.** tree planting
> **D.** donation　　**E.** helping children　　**F.** helping seniors

1 (　)

2 (　)

3 (　)

4 (　)

5 (　)

6 (　)

Reading A

The term is nearly over. One day when Li Ming and his classmates are studying hard for their final exams in the classroom, their head teacher Mr. Yang comes in with the president of the Students' Union. The president presents a poster and announces that the Students' Union is recruiting community volunteers. After that Mr. Yang strongly recommends this great chance and he shares with the whole class an article *Why is community service important* as below.

Pre-reading questions

1. Have you ever taken part in any community service?
2. Why should we take part in community service?

Why is community service important

Community service is one of the best ways to help benefit the public or give back to your community. It does not only have positive effects on the society, but it will bring benefits to your life and personal development. Why is community service important? If you have ever asked yourself this question, let's consider some of the possible reasons.

Community service helps connect to the community. Giving back and assisting others is the basis of community service or volunteering. Thus, it teaches us how significant it is to help the ones in need, the ones who are less fortunate than us. The importance of community service lies in the fact that it connects us to the community by improving it, and making it a better place for all of us to live in.

It benefits your career prospects. When you are thinking of changing or advancing your career, community service helps you gain experience and skills required for the professional turn you are considering taking. One of the community service benefits is that it provides you with the chance to improve skills important for a workplace, such as communication and organizational skills, teamwork, planning, problem-solving and task management. Furthermore, people could first merely try out an attractive career through volunteering before leaping to a long-term commitment.

Community service raises social awareness. How does volunteering benefit the community? Volunteering or community service provides you with a perfect opportunity to become closer to the community you live in. Community service broadens your horizons by helping you understand the needs of the society and the population you are trying to help through the project you are volunteering on. Reading or hearing about issues is not quite the same as getting personally involved. It brings you closer to families and individuals in need, gives you firsthand experience and understanding of the conditions they are in.

Community service establishes contacts and friendships. The easiest way to make friends is through activities you perform together. Not only would you be helping the ones in need, but you would also be able to meet some other volunteers. This benefit of community service is especially important if you are new in an area. After all, is there a better way to meet your neighbors and show them how eager you are to improve your community? In addition, you could invite your existing friends to do community service with you and through it, further strengthen your relationship and have fun at the same time.

Community service helps improve your skills. Introverts sometimes have problems meeting people and making friends. Volunteering might help shy and quiet individuals with this issue as it offers lots of opportunities to meet and work with various people. Thus, it is a valuable experience for improving and practicing how to socialize in diverse surroundings.

(470 words)

New words

*community	/kəˈmjuːnəti/	n.	社区；共同体
*benefit	/ˈbenɪfɪt/	v.	有益于，对……有益
		n.	利益，好处
*positive	/ˈpɒzətɪv/	a.	积极的；肯定的

*connect	/kəˈnekt/	v.	连接，连结
▲volunteer	/ˌvɒlənˈtɪə(r)/	n.	志愿者
		v.	自愿；做志愿者
*significant	/sɪɡˈnɪfɪkənt/	a.	有意义的
*fortunate	/ˈfɔːtʃənət/	a.	幸运的
*advance	/ədˈvɑːns/	v.	提升；促进；推进
▲organizational	/ˌɔːɡənaɪˈzeɪʃnəl/	a.	组织方面的
*merely	/ˈmɪəli/	ad.	仅仅
*leap	/liːp/	v.	跳跃；突然做
▲commitment	/kəˈmɪtmənt/	n.	承诺；(对工作或某活动)奉献，投入
▲awareness	/əˈweənəs/	n.	意识；认识
▲broaden	/ˈbrɔːdn/	v.	使扩大；使变宽
*horizon	/həˈraɪzn/	n.	地平线；视野；眼界
*issue	/ˈɪʃuː/	n.	问题
*involve	/ɪnˈvɒlv/	v.	牵涉；包含；使陷于
*individual	/ˌɪndɪˈvɪdʒuəl/	n.	个人，个体
*establish	/ɪˈstæblɪʃ/	v.	建立，创立
*perform	/pəˈfɔːm/	v.	执行；完成
firsthand	/ˈfɜːstˈhænd/	a.	第一手的；直接的；亲身的
▲existing	/ɪɡˈzɪstɪŋ/	a.	现存的；现有的
*strengthen	/ˈstreŋθn/	v.	加强；巩固
introvert	/ˈɪntrəvɜːt/	n.	内向的人
▲socialize	/ˈsəʊʃəlaɪz/	v.	交际；参与社交
▲diverse	/daɪˈvɜːs/	a.	不同的，多样的
▲surroundings	/səˈraʊndɪŋz/	n.	环境；周围的事物

💬 Phrases & expressions

give back to	回馈；回报；归还
have effect on	对……有影响
in need	贫困的；困难中的
lie in	在于
try out	尝试，实验
broaden one's horizons	开阔……的眼界
get involved	参与；介入
have problems doing something	做……有困难
community service	社区服务
organizational skill	组织能力
social awareness	社会意识

生词数	生词率	*B级词汇	*A级词汇	▲四、六级词汇	超纲词汇
27	5.74%	12	4	9	2

Notes

1. community service

Community service is unpaid work performed by a person or a group of people for the benefit and betterment of their community without any form of compensation. Community service can be distinct from volunteering, since it is not always performed on a voluntary basis and sometimes may be compulsory. Although personal benefits may be realized, it may be performed for a variety of reasons including citizenship requirements, a substitution of criminal justice sanctions, requirements of a school or a class, and requisites for the receipt of certain benefits.

2. volunteering

Volunteering is a voluntary act of an individual or a group freely giving time and labour for community service. Many volunteers are specifically trained in the areas they work, such as medicine, education, or emergency rescue. Others serve on an as-needed basis, such as in response to a natural disaster. Many schools on all education levels offer service-learning programs, which allow students to serve the community through volunteering while earning educational credits.

After-reading tasks

Task 1 Tick off the reasons why community service is important according to the passage.

☐ 1. to help connect to the community   ☐ 2. to benefit one's career prospects

☐ 3. to make one rich   ☐ 4. to establish contacts and friendships

☐ 5. to broaden one's horizons   ☐ 6. to raise social awareness

☐ 7. to help improve your skills   ☐ 8. to make one famous

Task 2 Read the passage again and decide whether the following statements are true (T) or false (F). If it is false, write the key words to support your answer.

( ) 1. Community service does not only bring benefits to the society, but it is good for our life and personal development.
_____
_____

( ) 2. Community service connects us to the community by improving it, and making it a better place for all of us to live in.
_____
_____

( ) 3. Community service helps us gain experience and money required for our career.
_____
_____

( ) 4. Community service broadens our horizons through some volunteering activities in some other communities than our own community.
_____
_____

( ) 5. Through community service, we can strengthen our relationship with our friends and have fun at the same time.
_____
_____

Listening and speaking

Task 1 After reading the article *Why is community service important*, Li Ming still hesitates to take part in it as he needs time to prepare for the final exams. So he decides to turn to his head teacher Mr. Yang for more information before making the final decision. Listen to Mr. Yang's introduction of "What is community service" three times and complete the following note.

Community service is often done near the	• _____ where you live.
Your own community gets the	• _____ of your work.
To do community service you do not get	• _____ but volunteer your _____.
Community service can help people like	• _____, senior citizens, people with disabilities.
Community service is often organized through	• a local _____, such as school.
Many people participate in community service	• because they enjoy _____ others and _____ their community.
Some students do community service in order to	• _____ from high school or to receive certain _____.

Unit 4 | Community Service

Task 2 To his surprise, Li Ming finds that Liu Heng, his monitor, has entered for the community service. He wonders why Liu Heng, who always puts his study before everything, will participate so quickly. He talks to Liu Heng after class. Listen to their conversation three times and choose the best answers to complete the following sentences.

1. This conversation most probably takes place _____.
   A. in the library   B. in the classroom   C. on the playground   D. in the dormitory
2. Li Ming feels hesitated to take part in the community service because of _____.
   A. no interest in it   B. no idea about it   C. the monitor   D. the final exams
3. Liu Heng believes that volunteering is a valuable experience for him to practice how to _____ in diverse environments.
   A. socialize   B. work   C. speak   D. help
4. The community service helps establish _____.
   A. the Students' Union   B. contacts and friendships   C. career center   D. volunteer center
5. The community service helps gain work experience and learn more about _____.
   A. certain people   B. certain things   C. certain jobs   D. certain skills

Task 3 After talking with Liu Heng, Li Ming calls his father to seek for support. He wonders how his father will ease his anxiety for the final exams and whether he will support him to volunteer his time to the community service. Listen to their conversation three times and fill in the blanks.

Li Ming: Hi, dad. What do you think of participating in the community service?

Father: A good thing! What troubles you, boy?

Li Ming: I know it is good. My teacher and my classmates all said it is ___1___ of doing. But I am so ___2___ about my final exams. I don't think I have enough time.

Father: My boy, remember you did learn how to manage time before. Use those skills right now! It is very important to calm down before doing any exam.

Li Ming: Oh, you remind me of time management. So, dad, do you really believe that I can do well both in the final exams and in the community service?

Father: Of course I do. Trust me, boy, you will be happy to do community service. It ___3___ you to the community by improving it, and making it a ___4___ place for all of us to live in.

Li Ming: I understand. It is important to help people in need.

Father: In addition to helping others, my boy, ___5___ awareness and responsibility are what I really hope you can ___6___ from community service. It helps you understand the needs of the society and the population. Getting personally involved gives you ___7___ experience and understanding of the conditions they are in.

Li Ming:	I will try my best. My teacher also says the community service benefits our career prospects. I remember we can gain work experience from on-campus training as well. Are they the same?	
Father:	Not exactly, although they are similar in improving skills important for a ___8___, such as communication skills, team work, problem-solving, etc. Compared with working within campus where is relatively safe and sound, community service provides you with environments where you may need to ___9___ with uncertainties.	
Li Ming:	That sounds ___10___.	
Father:	Yes. One day you will realize life is never easy. Why not go out and experience real life as early as possible?	
Li Ming:	OK, I will go. Thanks, dad.	

Task 4 In the office, Li Ming signs up for the community service and asks his head teacher Mr. Yang for more advice on how to get involved in the community service. Listen to their conversation three times and tick off the items mentioned.

☐	1. figure out how much money	☐	2. look over your interests
☐	3. vary from person to person	☐	4. available every weekend
☐	5. on a regular basis	☐	6. nursing home
☐	7. take volunteers	☐	8. take projects
☐	9. appreciate your work	☐	10. much larger projects

Task 5 Suppose you are Li Ming and your partner is the monitor Liu Heng. You tell each other which benefits you value most of doing the community service. Make up a dialogue and role-play it in class.

Task 6 The following are four kinds of community service. Discuss them with your partner, and then tell each other: Which one are you interested in? What activity did you once do? Tell the details. If you haven't done any activity, what activity do you plan to do? Why?

- Helping children and schools
- Helping senior citizens
- Helping animals and the environment
- Reducing crime and promoting safety

After leaving the office, Li Ming immediately reads through the e-copy of *List of community service* as below. He is eager to know what he can choose from the list to start to do some community service within his capability.

List of community service

Community service, also called community dedication, refers to work that is done without pay to help people in a community. Below are some community service ideas to get you started.

General ideas

- Donate or raise money for your local Red Cross
- Organize a community blood drive
- Read books or letters to a person who is actually impaired
- Participate in a charity race
- Volunteer to help at a charity auction
- Collect unused makeup and perfume to donate to a center for abused women
- Help deliver meals and gifts to patients at a local hospital

Helping children and schools

- Tutor children during or after school
- Collect used sports equipment to donate to families and after-school programs
- Volunteer at a summer camp for children who have lost a parent
- Put on performances for children in hospitals
- Become a volunteer teen crisis counselor
- Organize events to help new students make friends
- Donate used children's books to a school library

Helping senior citizens

- Deliver groceries and meals to elderly neighbors
- Teach computer skills to the elderly

- Organize a family day for people of a retirement home and relatives to play games together
- Pick up medicine for an elderly neighbor
- Perform a concert or play at a senior center
- Help elderly neighbors clean their homes and organize their belongings
- Deliver cookies to a homebound senior citizen

Helping animals and the environment

- Sponsor an animal at your local zoo
- Build and set up a bird house
- Clean up a local park
- Update the signs along a nature trail
- Participate in the cleanup of a local river, pond, or lake
- Organize a carpool to reduce car emissions
- Volunteer at a nature camp and teach kids about the environment

Helping the hungry and/or homeless

- Donate your old clothes, blankets to a homeless shelter
- Volunteer at a soup kitchen
- Donate non-perishable food to a food bank
- Make "care kits" with shampoo, toothbrushes, combs, etc. to donate to a homeless shelter
- Donate art supplies to kids in a homeless shelter
- Help organize and sort donations at a homeless shelter
- Make first aid kits for a homeless shelter

Reducing crime and promoting safety

- Become a certified lifeguard and volunteer at a local pool or beach
- Paint over graffiti in your neighborhood
- Organize a self-defense workshop
- Organize a drug-free campaign
- Start or join a neighborhood watch program
- Teach a home-alone safety class for children
- Volunteer as a crossing guard for an elementary school

Promoting community enhancement

- Donate used books to your local library
- Plant flowers in bare public areas
- Organize a campaign to raise money to buy and install new playground equipment for a park
- Campaign for more lighting along poorly lit streets
- Volunteer to clean up trash at a community event
- Adopt a local highway or road and clean up trash along it
- Help fix or raise funds to repair a run-down playground

(477 words)

Unit 4 | Community Service

New words

▲donate	/dəʊˈneɪt/	v.	捐赠，捐献
impair	/ɪmˈpeə/	v.	损害
▲charity	/ˈtʃærəti/	n.	慈善机构（或组织）；慈善；赈济；博爱
▲auction	/ˈɔːkʃn/	n.	拍卖
▲makeup	/ˈmeɪkʌp/	n.	化妆品；组成
▲perfume	/ˈpɜːfjuːm/	n.	香水；香味
▲abuse	/əˈbjuːz/	v.	虐待；滥用
*tutor	/ˈtjuːtə(r)/	v.	辅导；当指导教师
		n.	家庭教师；指导教师；导师
▲counselor	/ˈkaʊnsələ(r)/	n.	顾问；法律顾问
▲grocery	/ˈɡrəʊsəri/	n.	食品杂货店；食品杂货
▲belongings	/bɪˈlɒŋɪŋz/	n.	财产，所有物
homebound	/ˈhəʊmbaʊnd/	a.	回家的，回家乡的
*sponsor	/ˈspɒnsə(r)/	v.	赞助；发起；主办
▲update	/ˌʌpˈdeɪt/	v.	更新
carpool	/ˈkɑːpuːl/	n.	合伙用车者；拼车
*reduce	/rɪˈdjuːs/	v.	减少；缩小
▲emission	/ɪˈmɪʃn/	n.	排放；排放物
*shelter	/ˈʃeltə(r)/	n.	庇护；避难所
perishable	/ˈperɪʃəbl/	a.	（食物等）易腐烂的；易变质的
		n.	易腐品；非耐用品
▲kit	/kɪt/	n.	成套设备；全套衣服及装备
shampoo	/ʃæmˈpuː/	n.	洗发水；香波
*sort	/sɔːt/	v.	将……分类；整理
▲donation	/dəʊˈneɪʃn/	n.	捐款，捐赠
▲certify	/ˈsɜːtɪfaɪ/	v.	证明；保证
graffiti	/ɡrəˈfiːti/	n.	墙上乱写乱画的东西（graffito的复数形式）
*bare	/beə(r)/	a.	空的；赤裸的，无遮蔽的
*campaign	/kæmˈpeɪn/	n.	运动；活动
▲trash	/træʃ/	n.	垃圾；废物
run-down	/ˌrʌn ˈdaʊn/	a.	破败的；衰弱的

Phrases & expressions

clean up	清扫；清理，清除
Red Cross	红十字会
community blood drive	社区献血活动
charity race	慈善比赛
charity auction	慈善拍卖
retirement home	养老院；敬老院
senior center	老年中心；老年活动中心
car emissions	汽车尾气
soup kitchen	流动厨房；贫民救济处
food bank	食物银行；食物储蓄站
care kit	护理包
homeless shelter	无家可归者收留所
first aid kit	急救包
certified lifeguard	注册救生员
crossing guard	交通管理员
elementary school	小学

生词数	生词率	*B级词汇	*A级词汇	▲四、六级词汇	超纲词汇
30	6.29%	3	5	15	7

After-reading tasks

Task 1 Match the English phrases in the left column with their Chinese equivalents in the right column.

(　) 1. retirement home　　A. 急救包
(　) 2. first aid kit　　B. 无家可归者收留所
(　) 3. homeless shelter　　C. 汽车尾气
(　) 4. crossing guard　　D. 注册救生员
(　) 5. charity auction　　E. 老年中心
(　) 6. car emissions　　F. 社区献血活动
(　) 7. community blood drive　　G. 交通管理员
(　) 8. certified lifeguard　　H. 慈善拍卖
(　) 9. soup kitchen　　I. 养老院
(　) 10. senior center　　J. 贫民救济处

Task 2 Translate the following passage into Chinese.

List of community service

Helping children and schools

- Tutor children during or after school.
- Put on performances for children in hospitals.
- Become a volunteer teen crisis counselor.

Helping senior citizens

- Deliver groceries and meals to elderly neighbors.
- Pick up medicine for an elderly neighbor.
- Deliver cookies to a homebound senior citizen.

Helping the hungry and/or homeless

- Volunteer at a soup kitchen.
- Donate non-perishable food to a food bank.
- Make first aid kits for a homeless shelter.

Promoting community enhancement

- Donate used books to your local library.
- Plant flowers in bare public areas.
- Volunteer to clean up trash at a community event.

Comprehensive exercises

Task 1 Fill in the blanks with the words or expressions from Readings A and B according to the meanings in the right column. The first letter of each word is already given to help your spelling. Then compare your answers with your partner.

v_____	to offer to do something willingly without being paid for it or without being asked to do it
i_____	to have as a part or result
d_____	many and different
d_____	to give money or goods to help a person or an organization
s_____	to pay for someone to do something or for something to happen
u_____	to make something more modern by adding new parts, etc.
p_____ _____	to perform or organize a show, exhibition, or service
t_____	to test something in order to find out how useful or effective it is or what it is like
g_____	to return something to the person who gave it to you
p_____ _____	to gather or collect

Task 2 Complete the following sentences with the words and expressions from Task 1. Change the form if necessary.

1. Some car buyers hope to _____ the car in the street before they make a decision.
2. Since it has been raining for weeks and no one knows exactly when it stops, we have to _____ our schedule for the sports meet.
3. Customers may be willing to buy a company's products as an indirect way to _____ to the charity causes it helps.
4. I am wondering whether you can _____ my suit from the cleaner's when you go home after work.
5. As a successful businessman, Mr. Clinton believes that it is his duty to _____ to the community.
6. In many cities such as Guangzhou and Shenzhen, a(n) _____ and growing economy has offered more job opportunities for college graduates.
7. The company plans to _____ more television programs as part of its marketing campaign.
8. The team _____ an excellent show in the competition and finally became the biggest winner.
9. Being a sailor _____ being away from home and family members for a long time.
10. She now helps in a local library as a(n) _____ three days a week.

Task 3 Complete the following sentences with the appropriate forms of the words given in the brackets.

1. It is important that students develop an _____ (aware) of how the Internet can be used properly.
2. Parents should let the children themselves decide with whom they want to _____ (society) and make friends.
3. Please make sure you have all your _____ (belong) with you when leaving the plane.
4. When cleaning up the room Mary found some goods in the corner which had been left _____ (use) and forgotten for long.
5. Cycling is good exercise. It _____ (strong) all the muscles of the body.
6. When talking about the benefits of travel, I strongly believe that few people would disagree that it _____ (broad) the mind.
7. The development of 5G technology helps to take the mobile phones' _____ (perform) a big leap forward.
8. It was _____ (fortune) that he wasn't injured in the accident.
9. A recent study shows there are _____ (significance) differences among women based on ages, places of residence, and educational levels.
10. It's not the knowledge that is _____ (value) but the practice of learning new things and understanding how things work.

Task 4 Rewrite the following sentences according to the examples.

Example 1: Sometimes *it is difficult for introverts to meet people and make friends*.
→Introverts sometimes *have problems meeting people and making friends*.

1. Generally speaking, it is difficult for left-handers to use can-openers, scissors, and dust catchers.
   _____

2. It's quite difficult for people over 50 to remember the names of other people, places, and things quickly.
   _____

3. They admit that it is very difficult for them to bring up four kids during the hard times.
   _____

4. With increasing environmental pollution, it is difficult for millions of people to get clean and safe water.
   _____

5. Although I set my alarm clock every day, it is still difficult for me to get out of bed and go to work on time.
   _____

Example 2: *You would not only be helping* the ones in need, but you would also be able to meet some other volunteers.

→ *Not only would you be helping* the ones in need, but you would also be able to meet some other volunteers.

1. We can create or destroy energy by no means.
   _____

2. We seldom go for picnics as we live in the city.
   _____

3. Wood does not conduct electricity, and rubber doesn't either.
   _____

4. Exercise will not only lower blood pressure but possibly protect against heart attacks.
   _____

5. The mathematician spoke about his research for two hours, but we cannot understand a word.
   _____

Task 5 Complete the following English sentences using the words or phrases given in the brackets.

1. Riding a bicycle is _____ (减少汽车排放量和空气污染的好办法). Thus, it _____ (对……有积极的作用) environmental protection. (a way to, reduce car emissions, have an effect on)

2. By _____ (参与社区服务), we can _____ (获得一手的生活经验), make more friends and _____ (提高社会意识). (get involved in, gain firsthand experience, raise social awareness)

3. _____ (已经募集了资金) as part of the campaign for _____ (在附近建立一所养老院). (raise money, a retirement home, in the neighborhood)

4. It's important _____ (理解社会需求和个人兴趣) before starting your job hunt and consider what experience and skills of yours _____ (会有利于你的职业前景). (the needs of the society, personal interests, benefit, career prospects)

5. His tutor encouraged him to read widely and _____ (多与各种人交流), which helps to _____ (开阔眼界和提高交际能力). (socialize with, broaden one's horizons, communication skills)

Applied writing

海报

海报是一种常见的招贴形式，多用于电影、戏剧、比赛、文艺演出、商品报道等，其性质类似于宣传，有的还配以绘画来增加吸引力。海报通常要写清楚活动的性质、主办单位、时间、地点等内容。语言应简明扼要，形式要灵活多样，力求新颖美观。阅读下面的海报样例，了解海报的写作特点。

Sample

Volunteers Wanted

Do you want to be a volunteer for the 2008 Beijing Olympic Games? We are really in great need of volunteers. If you want to apply for this position, you are required to:

☆ speak good English   ☆ be friendly

☆ know about the games   ☆ enjoy helping people

Call the Organizing Committee (组委会) of the 2008 Beijing Olympic Games at 66699999 for more information.

Writing task

Li Ming is going to apply for a post as a volunteer in fighting against the COVID-19 in Guangzhou. You are required to write an English poster according to the Chinese information given below.

核酸检测志愿者招募

一、服务时间：5月31日

二、服务地点：广东轻工职业技术学院核酸检测点

三、服务内容

1. 协助医护人员维持核酸检测现场秩序
2. 协助待检测人员填写个人资料登记表

四、招募要求

1. 年龄18周岁以上
2. 身心健康，无重大疾病史，14天内无中高风险地区旅居史
3. 抗压能力、应变能力强
4. 已经注射2剂疫苗者优先
5. 穗康码和粤康码均呈绿码

五、志愿者保障

1. 提供口罩、防护面罩、洗手液等防护物资
2. 志愿者服装或标记
3. 志愿服务证明
4. 提供饮用水

六、报名方式

识别下方二维码加入海珠区疫情防控志愿者微信群

Words for reference

1. 核酸检测 Nucleic Acid Test
2. 医护人员 medical personnel
3. 权益保障 benefit guarantee
4. 维持秩序 keep order
5. 穗康码 Suikang code
6. 粤康码 Yuekang code
7. 二维码 QR Code/two-dimensional barcode
8. 中高风险地区 the medium- and high-risk areas
9. 志愿服务证明 volunteer certificate

Unit 4 | Community Service

Project performing

💬 Guidelines

This project aims to simulate relevant situations of conducting community service. The whole task is divided into three steps. Step one is about trying to figure out the importance of community service. Step two focuses on deciding on necessary community service. Step three is concerned with writing a poster in the community.

Please follow the task description to complete the project.

Task description

Step one

- Organize a small group of 4 to 6 students in your class;
- Brainstorm and share the importance of community service;
- Give a presentation to introduce the effect of community service on future career.

Step two

- List as many community service ideas as possible that your community can offer;
- Divide the group into two sides: One side is community officers, the other is volunteers;
- Take turns to play roles: The side of community officers announces what kind of community service is needed, and the other side shows what kind of community service they can do.

Step three

- The side of community officers asks for more volunteers to do community service, and the side of volunteers writes a poster accordingly;
- Discuss the poster with group members;
- Give a presentation to the whole class about your poster.

Grammar

进行时态的基本用法和特殊用法

1. 现在进行时

基本用法/特殊用法	例句
表示现在正在进行的动作和发生的事，有时表示现阶段正发生的事情	Mary is knitting and listening to the radio. I'm waiting to have a word with you. I'm writing a book about ecology.
在口语中可表示将来的动作，指已计划或安排好的事情，后面接表示未来时间的状语	He's flying to Hong Kong tomorrow. They are getting married next month.
在时间或条件状语从句中，用现在进行时表示未来的情况	You must visit Switzerland when you are travelling in Europe. If she's still waiting, tell her to go home.
表示经常性的动作，常和always, constantly, forever等副词连用，表示赞美或厌烦等情绪	He is always losing his keys. You are always thinking of others. She's constantly making that mistake.

2. 过去进行时

基本用法/特殊用法	例句
表示一个动作在过去某个时间正在进行；也可用在状语从句中，表示当过去另一件事发生时正在进行的动作	I was writing a letter when she called. At that moment, I wasn't doing anything. He met the bride while he was studying in California.
表示过去某个时间打算要做的事情或预计要发生的事情，常用于come, go, leave这类动词	She told me she was going to Boston. He was busy packing, for he was leaving that night.
表示过去反复或经常发生的动作或状态，常和always, constantly, forever等频度副词连用，表达说话人的感情色彩	He was always ringing me up. She was always working. The old lady was forever grumbling.
表示客气的询问	I was wondering if you could give me a lift.

3. 将来进行时

基本用法/特殊用法	例句
表示将来某个时间将正在进行的动作	This time tomorrow we'll be sitting in the cinema and watching a film. A space vehicle will be circling Jupiter in five years' time.
表示安排要做的事情或预计会发生的事情	He'll be taking his exam next week. We'll be getting in touch with you.

Task 1 Complete the following sentences using proper forms of the given verbs.

1. —What are you doing?
   —I _____ (read) a play by Shaw.
2. I'm meeting Peter tonight. He _____ (take) me to the theatre.
3. Suppose it _____ (still rain) tomorrow, shall we go?
4. The baby _____ (constantly scream).
5. It _____ (rain) hard all afternoon.
6. We _____ (have) supper when the phone rang.
7. While I was working in the garden, my wife _____ (cook) dinner.
8. Next Wednesday we _____ (fly) to Sydney.
9. He _____ (work) at the moment, so he can't come to the telephone.
10. People _____ (become) less tolerant of smoking these days.

Task 2 Choose the best answer to complete each of the following sentences.

1. —Who _____?
   —_____ to get through Helen.
   A. do you phone; I'm trying   B. are you phoning; I'm trying
   C. are you phoning; I try   D. do you phone; I try

2. When he realized I _____ at him, he _____ away.
   A. looked; was turning   B. was looking; turned
   C. was looking; was turning   D. looked; turned

3. When the builders were here, I _____ them cups of tea all the time.
   A. was making   B. am making   C. was made   D. make

4. We _____ a party next Saturday. Can you come?
   A. are to have   B. are having   C. have   D. are have

5. This time next year this part of the garden _____ beautiful.
   A. was looking   B. is looking   C. looks   D. will be looking

6. After the operation you _____ any sport for a while.
   A. won't be doing   B. aren't doing   C. don't do   D. won't to do

7. We _____ each other later that day, but I had to phone and cancel.
   A. see   B. are seeing   C. were seeing   D. saw

8. Tony is a kind person. He _____ always _____ to help me with my work.
   A. is going to; offer   B. is; offering   C. was; offering   D. will; offer

9. She _____ the 1,500 meters in the next Olympics.
   A. is run   B. runs   C. is to run   D. is running

10. I lived in France at that time you _____ in Spain.
    A. are living   B. live   C. were living D. will be living

Task 3 Translate the following sentences into English.

1. 昨天我很忙，我在准备考试。
2. 到明天这个时间，我将正在海滩上躺着。
3. 她老是改变主意。
4. 你等火车时可以看看书。
5. 不知你能否帮我出点主意。

Self-evaluation

Rate your own progress in this unit.	D	M	P	F*
I can say words and expressions about community service in English.	☐	☐	☐	☐
I can tell the importance of community service.	☐	☐	☐	☐
I can know how to join in community service.	☐	☐	☐	☐
I can choose from a list of community service.	☐	☐	☐	☐
I can write a poster.	☐	☐	☐	☐
I can master usages of continuous tenses.	☐	☐	☐	☐

*Note: D (Distinction), M (Merit), P (Pass), F (Fail)

Culture

社会公益事业是中国优良传统的延续，是构建社会主义和谐社会的内在要求。公益活动的内容包括社区服务、环境保护、知识传播、公共福利、帮助他人、社会援助、社会治安、紧急援助、青年服务、慈善、社团活动、专业服务、文化艺术活动、国际合作等。

公益活动几乎都是由单位或学校等各个机构组织的，如义务植树、义务大扫除、爱心满世界志愿者、献血、捐款（物）、爱心助学、关爱失独等。这些公益活动都是一份爱心，不仅有益于改善我们的生存环境，而且给需要帮助的人们带去了一份希望。

 Watch the following video clip, and then complete the passage with missing words and phrases.

My volunteering life in Beijing

Hello, I'm Maria from Bolivia, and I'm a resident in Sugar Bay Community and also a volunteer. Our work mostly includes making sure that everybody that comes in has their ____1____ taken and healthy enough to come into the community. Many reasons actually to ____2____. The main reason why I decided to volunteer is because I was really ____3____ the hard work that all of the volunteers did. So I wanted to do anything to support them and provide my help, and also practice my Chinese. I know there are a lot of foreigners living in this community. So I thought volunteering was going to be a good thing for me and for everybody who lives here. I'm really glad that I had the chance to get to know my neighbors better and I had a chance to volunteer and work together with my ____4____ and support and help my community. I think the way that China has contained the virus is being extremely smart and very ____5____. I feel safe living in Beijing. I think China did a great job containing the virus in general.

 Discuss in groups the community service you have taken part in and make a presentation to introduce it to your friends.

Unit 5
Post Internships

Learning objectives

After studying this unit, you should be able to:
- get familiar with the words and expressions concerning post internships;
- understand the types of post internships;
- know more about post internships and how to get involved in them;
- be clear about the ways to find an internship;
- master the skills of writing a job description;
- be expert at the usages of perfect tenses.

Warm-up

Task 1 Watch the video and answer the following questions orally. Some key words and phrases are listed for you.

assessment 评估；评定	assessed internship 评估实习
competency-based 基于能力的	mentor 导师
supervisor 主管；监督员	review 评审；审查

1. What are the FIVE steps to a career on Shell Graduate Programme via the internship route?
2. What does the online assessment include?
3. Who will guide the interns through the assessed internship?
4. How many reviews are there in the assessed internship?

Task 2 Look at the poster and answer the following questions orally.

1. What is the application deadline for 2021 internships?
2. To whom are these internship positions open?
3. How many internship positions are available?
4. What does "FALL" mean here?

Reading A

The department plans to hold a meeting to promote internships among the senior students. Mrs. Li, the Dean of the Department, hosts the meeting. Before the meeting, Mrs. Li shares with the students an article *Types of student internships* as below. Li Ming shows great interest in the article and the promotion meeting.

Pre-reading questions

1. Have you ever taken part in any internship program?
2. What types of internships do you know?

Types of student internships

Whether or not you'll get paid for your internship is probably the most frequently asked question by college students looking for internship placements. After all, haven't we been told never to work for free? But internships are a little bit different, and follow a different set of rules than regular employment, and a successful internship usually has nothing to do with whether or not you are being paid.

There are essentially two kinds of internships: paid and for-credit. In the corporate worlds of finance, real estate and law, paid internships are common, and some pay as much as an entry level position. Typically the higher the pay, the more competitive the internship becomes. In the world of not-for-profit, education and arts, internships are generally unpaid, but will offer credits towards graduation.

High-paying internships are not only competitive to obtain, but can also be competitive in the workplace. If you are thinking about your internship as a long job interview, those that are high paying have a higher likelihood of turning into full-time jobs than those that are for credit. After all, the company you work for has already made a large investment by hiring someone without experience, and has spent a significant amount of time as well as money training you. It is important to realize that even if an internship is paid, you should treat it as more than just a job, and go out of your way to do your best work every day to not only earn a paycheck, but to get noticed by the people in charge. Typically, a company will have fewer open positions than they do interns, and each intern will be vying for the same full-time spot.

This is not to say that for-credit internships do not lead to employment. In fact, many for-credit internships, specifically those that actively recruit through the university career services department, will be looking for the best and brightest students to groom through internships, but will also want to see what kind of commitment they show to the organization without a paycheck. For that reason, it is important to treat your for-credit internship position as a paid internship.

It is also essential that you make sure that your college or university accepts credit for an internship. In some cases you may have to get sponsorship from a professor or the chairperson of the academic department. Just don't assume that you can credit after you've already completed the internship, as this is rarely the case.

Of course, for many people getting paid is an absolute necessity. If this is the case and you cannot find a paid internship in your field, you might want to consider getting a corporate internship. While this internship may not be a direct path to your professional goals, any work experience can ultimately prepare you for a career.

(487 words)

New words

▲frequently	/ˈfriːkwəntli/	ad.	频繁地；经常地；屡次
*regular	/ˈreɡjələ(r)/	a.	有规律的，定时的；经常的
*essentially	/ɪˈsenʃəli/	ad.	本质上；基本上
*credit	/ˈkredɪt/	n.	学分
		v.	获得学分
▲corporate	/ˈkɔːpərət/	a.	公司的；企业的
*estate	/ɪˈsteɪt/	n.	大片私有土地；住宅区
*entry	/ˈentri/	n.	进入；入口
*typically	/ˈtɪpɪkli/	ad.	典型地；通常；一贯地
▲graduation	/ˌɡrædʒuˈeɪʃn/	n.	毕业
not-for-profit	/ˌnɒt fə ˈprɒfɪt/	a.	非赢（营）利的
high-paying	/ˈhaɪ ˈpeɪɪŋ/	a.	高薪的
*competitive	/kəmˈpetətɪv/	a.	竞争的；好胜的；有竞争力的
▲likelihood	/ˈlaɪklihʊd/	n.	可能性，可能
*investment	/ɪnˈvestmənt/	n.	投资；投入
intern	/ˈɪntɜːn/	n.	实习生
		v.	实习；做实习生
vie	/vaɪ/	v.	激烈竞争；争夺

groom	/gruːm/	v.	使做好准备；培养
paycheck	/ˈpeɪtʃek/	n.	薪水
▲sponsorship	/ˈspɒnsəʃɪp/	n.	赞助；支持
▲chairperson	/ˈtʃeəpɜːsn/	n.	主席
*assume	/əˈsjuːm/	v.	假定，设想
▲absolute	/ˈæbsəluːt/	a.	绝对的
▲necessity	/nəˈsesəti/	n.	必然性；必需品
▲ultimately	/ˈʌltɪmətli/	ad.	最后；根本；基本上

💬 Phrases & expressions

have nothing to do with	与……无关
go out of one's way to do something	尽力做……
vie for	争夺……；竞争……
be the case	是这样；是这种情况
real estate	房地产
entry level position	初级职位
job interview	求职面试
full-time job	全职工作
people in charge	负责人
open position	空缺职位
university career services department	大学就业服务中心
corporate internship	公司实习

生词数	生词率	*B级词汇	*A级词汇	▲四、六级词汇	超纲词汇
25	5.13%	4	5	9	7

📑 Notes

1. internship

An internship is a period of work experience offered by an organization for a limited period of time. Internship is used for a wide range of placements in businesses, non-profit organizations and government agencies. They are typically undertaken by students and graduates looking to gain relevant skills and experience in a particular field. Employers benefit from these placements because they often recruit employees from their best interns, who have known capabilities, thus saving time and money in the long run. Internships are usually arranged by third-party organizations that recruit interns on behalf of industry groups. Rules vary from country to country about when interns should be regarded as employees. The system can be open to exploitation by unscrupulous employers.

2. university career services department

Most colleges and universities have a career services department, which may be alternatively called a career center, career placement office, or career office. Regardless of the name, this office provides a variety of services to help students (and often alumni) meet that goal. Here are some basic services you can expect from your college's Career Services Office. 1. Career Decision Making: A counselor at the Career Services Office can help you choose a career, whether you have no idea about what you want to do or are leaning toward a particular occupation; 2. Recruiting: Career Services Offices host job fairs during which employers visit the campus to recruit students who are about to graduate; 3. Internships: While there's probably a separate office that handles internships, career counseling centers often work hand in hand with companies seeking college interns and internship advisers.

After-reading tasks

Task 1 Read the passage and fill in the blanks with appropriate information from the passage.

There are essentially ___1___ kinds of internships: paid and for-credit. In the corporate worlds of finance, real estate and law, ___2___ are common, and some pay as much as an ___3___ position. Typically the higher the pay, the more ___4___ the internship becomes. In the world of not-for-profit, education and arts, internships are generally unpaid, but will offer ___5___ towards graduation.

Task 2 Read the passage again and decide whether the following statements are true (T) or false (F). If it is false, write the key words to support your answer.

(　　) 1. In the corporate worlds of finance, real estate and law, internships are commonly paid but offer no credits towards graduation.

(　　) 2. In the world of not-for-profit, education and arts, internships are generally unpaid, but will offer credits towards graduation.

(　　) 3. Typically each intern will be vying for the same full-time spot, because a company will have fewer open positions than they do interns.

(　　) 4. Generally speaking, for-credit internships do not lead to employment.

(　　) 5. Once you've already completed the internship, you are sure to get credits.

Listening and speaking

Task 1

After reading the article *Types of student internships*, Li Ming understands two different kinds of internships. However, the article doesn't show him what is an internship and why college students must do internships. At the end of the promotion meeting, Li Ming puts up his hand to ask questions. Listen to Mrs. Li's responses three times and complete the following note.

An internship is an opportunity offered by an	• _____ to potential employees to work in a company.
Internships can be as short as a	• _____ or as long as 12 months.
Reason 1: Employers want to see	• _____ in the new graduates they _____.
Reason 2: You may get	• _____ more when you graduate if you've done one or more internships.
Reason 3: You will gain better	• understanding of your _____ field.
Reason 4: You will	• _____ many workplace skills. If you're afraid of facing the _____ world, an internship will teach you that you can do it.
Reason 5: You will	• _____ your _____ and your résumé.

Task 2 After leaving the meeting hall, Li Ming and Liu Heng, his monitor, have a hot discussion on different kinds of internships on the way back to the classroom. Listen to their conversation three times and choose the best answers to complete the following sentences.

1. High-paying internships are more likely to turn into _____.
   A. full-time jobs   B. part-time jobs   C. voluntary jobs   D. temporary jobs

2. Internships that pay well are usually _____.
   A. the most interesting   B. the most difficult
   C. the most useful   D. the most competitive

3. Doing a voluntary internship, we can at least test out _____ in our major or interests.
   A. study paths   B. career paths   C. research paths   D. internship program

4. It is important to treat a _____ as a paid one.
   A. long-term internship   B. for-credit internship
   C. short-term internship   D. voluntary internship

5. It will be better for Li Ming and Liu Heng to check first with the Career Services Office to see _____.
   A. their company's policies   B. their opportunities
   C. their department's policies   D. their requirements

Task 3 The next day, Li Ming and Liu Heng go to the Career Services Office to consult about the internship policies, and furthermore about how to get an internship. Mr. Wang, one of the advisers in the office, meets them warmly. Listen to their conversation three times and fill in the blanks.

Li Ming: Hello, Mr. Wang. We wonder what our department's policies are on ___1___.

Mr. Wang: I am happy to help. What do you need to know?

Li Ming: We are interested in for-credit internships. We want to make sure whether our department ___2___ credit for an internship.

Mr. Wang: It depends. If you do paid internships in the field of finance, real estate and law, your department will not offer credits. It will only offer if you do the unpaid internships in ___3___ and arts, the work world of not-for-profit.

Li Ming: What if I do an unpaid internship in the industry like hotel management?

Mr. Wang: The policy doesn't state that your department accepts credit for an internship in hotel management.

Li Ming: I see. In addition to this issue, we need advice on how to get an internship.

Mr. Wang: Use the following steps to ___4___ you. First of all, you'll need to decide what you're looking for in an internship. Then you can move on to the next step: begin your internship search.

Li Ming: What shall we do in this step?

Mr. Wang: You can use online search. You can narrow those searches by location and industry to find something that suits your ___5___ and interests. Once you've found the right internship, start applying.

Li Ming: Start by ___6___ my résumé?

Mr. Wang: Yes. Make sure you ___7___ any relevant skills and refer to the job posting to ___8___ what they are looking for.

Li Ming: What if it's been a few weeks and I haven't ___9___ back from the company?

Mr. Wang: Call or email the hiring ___10___. If they offer you a chance, next, prepare for the internship interview. For example, you can search for common interview questions for the position and practice interviewing.

Li Ming: Mr. Wang, thank you so much for your time and advice.

Mr. Wang: You are welcome. Hope these can help.

Task 4 Mr. Wang, one of the advisers in the Career Services Office, explains how to get an internship for Li Ming and Liu Heng. However, Li Ming is not confident at all in finding internships. He needs more advice on how to find an internship so he talks to Mrs. Li, the Dean of the Department, to seek for help. Listen to their conversation three times and tick off the items mentioned.

☐ 1. start your search late	☐ 2. start your search early
☐ 3. learn communicating	☐ 4. take advantage of social media
☐ 5. learn networking	☐ 6. take advantage of news media
☐ 7. informational interviews	☐ 8. job interviews
☐ 9. going to job fairs	☐ 10. screen and hire talented interns

Task 5 Some students prefer high-paying internship, while others prefer low workload internship. What do you prefer? Why? Make a speech on it in class.

Task 6 Which way do you prefer to use for finding internships, online or offline? Suppose you are Li Ming and your partner is the monitor Liu Heng. Work in pairs. Make up a dialogue to explain your choice and role-play it in the class.

The Dean of the Department sends Li Ming an article *6 ways to find an internship* as below. He reads it through carefully. He wants to learn more ways so as to start to look for an internship for himself.

6 ways to find an internship

You stand the best chance of finding the perfect internship if you employ several different strategies. Finding an internship requires time and planning, but the results are definitely worth the effort. Here are some recommendations for those seeking a successful internship.

Start your search early

Be aware that certain industries and internships have early deadlines and recruit and hire as early as November. Beginning your internship search during winter break affords you additional lead time. It can also give you the opportunity to make valuable connections with alumni or professionals within organizations of interest prior to returning to college. You can check with your college's Career Services Office for assistance and to find out which internships recruit early.

Identify your broad career interests

Decide what you want to do, but don't worry about being too specific. Gaining experience in a number of career fields is a good idea if you are unsure about the career you want to pursue after college. Think about what you enjoy and how that might parlay into a career. Do you enjoy watching shows on finance and investing? Home improvement? History? Are you interested in social activism and making a difference in the world? Internships can give you exposure to opportunities and a chance to sample new and exciting career fields.

Network

Speak with family, friends, faculty, college advisors, and career counselors in the Career Services Office at your college about what type of internship you want and when and where you want to do it. Contacting alumni from your college and doing informational interviews can provide you with valuable information on career options and internships that you can pursue. Be sure to send a thank-you note to them for sharing their time and expertise.

Check online resources

Contact the Career Services Office at your college to see if they have recommended internship resources that you might use or subscribe to. Internships.com specializes in internships only and is a good place to begin your search. Also visit company websites and online and offline classified ads to identify employers who may be interested in hiring an intern.

Attend career fairs

Check with the Career Services Office at your college to identify career and/or internship fairs occurring during winter break. Top employers attend career fairs to recruit, screen, and hire talented interns and employees. Be prepared to give a 60-second introduction that describes how you can be of value to an employer. Be sure to follow up with any recruiters you meet at a fair.

Contact employers

Telephone or visit employers in your geographic and/or career areas of interest and inquire about summer jobs/internships. Again, be prepared to give a 60-second introduction that sells skills and explains how you can be of value.

(467 words)

New words

*strategy	/ˈstrætədʒi/	n.	战略，策略
*recommendation	/ˌrekəmenˈdeɪʃn/	n.	推荐；建议；推荐信
*seek	/siːk/	v.	寻找；寻求；谋求
▲deadline	/ˈdedlaɪn/	n.	最终期限
*additional	/əˈdɪʃənl/	a.	附加的，额外的
alumni	/əˈlʌmnaɪ/	n.	校友；毕业生（alumnus的复数）
*professional	/prəˈfeʃənl/	n.	专业人员；职业运动员
*prior	/ˈpraɪə(r)/	a.	先前的；优先的
*identify	/aɪˈdentɪfaɪ/	v.	确定；鉴定；识别
parlay	/ˈpɑːleɪ/	v.	使增值；充分利用
*invest	/ɪnˈvest/	v.	投资；覆盖；耗费

activism	/ˈæktɪvɪzəm/	n.	行动主义;激进主义
▲sample	/ˈsɑːmpl/	n.	样品,样本;(化验的)抽样
		v.	品尝;体验
▲faculty	/ˈfæklti/	n.	全体教员
*contact	/ˈkɒntækt/	n.	联系;触摸
		v.	联系,与……交往
▲option	/ˈɒpʃn/	n.	选项;选择权;买卖的特权
▲expertise	/ˌekspɜːˈtiːz/	n.	专门知识;专门技术
▲subscribe	/səbˈskraɪb/	v.	订阅;认购
*specialize	/ˈspeʃəlaɪz/	v.	专门从事;详细说明;特化
*offline	/ˌɒfˈlaɪn/	a.	未联网的;脱机的
*classify	/ˈklæsɪfaɪ/	v.	分类;分等
*screen	/skriːn/	n.	屏幕;屏风
		v.	筛选;审查
▲talented	/ˈtæləntɪd/	a.	有才能的;多才的
▲recruiter	/rɪˈkruːtə(r)/	n.	招聘人员;征兵人员
*geographic	/ˌdʒɪəˈɡræfɪk/	a.	地理(上)的;地区(性)的

Phrases & expressions

stand a chance of doing…	有机会做……
make connections with…	关联,联系
prior to	在……之前
making a difference	有影响
subscribe to	定期订购(或订阅等)
specialize in	专门研究(从事);专攻
be of value	有积极作用,有意义
lead time	提前期;前置时间
Career Services Office	就业服务中心
career fields	职业领域
college advisor	大学指导老师
career counselor	职业咨询师
career options	职业选择
classified ads	分类广告
career fairs	招聘会

生词数	生词率	*B级词汇	*A级词汇	▲四、六级词汇	超纲词汇
25	5.35%	11	3	8	3

After-reading tasks

Task 1 Choose the right answers from A to J to match the information given in the table, and write them down in the answer column.

Information about finding an internship	Answer
Finding an internship	
Contacting alumni from your college and doing informational interviews	
Gaining experience in a number of career fields	
Beginning your internship search during winter break	
Speak with career counselors in the Career Services Office at your college	
Contact the Career Services Office at your college	
Visit company websites and online and offline classified ads	
Check with the Career Services Office at your college	
Be prepared to give a 60-second introduction	
Telephone or visit employers in your geographic and/or career areas of interest	

A. can provide you with valuable information on career options and internships.

B. requires time and planning, but the results are definitely worth the effort.

C. about what type of internship you want and when and where you want to do it.

D. that describes how you can be of value to an employer.

E. is a good idea if you are unsure about the career you want to pursue after college.

F. to see if they have recommended internship resources.

G. and inquire about summer jobs/internships.

H. to identify career and/or internship fairs occurring during winter break.

I. to identify employers who may be interested in hiring an intern.

J. give you the opportunity to make valuable connections with alumni.

Task 2 Translate the following paragraph into Chinese.

Decide what you want to do, but don't worry about being too specific. Gaining experience in a number of career fields is a good idea if you are unsure about the career you want to pursue after college. Think about what you enjoy and how that might parlay into a career. Do you enjoy watching shows on finance and investing? Home improvement? History? Are you interested in social activism and making a difference in the world? Internships can give you exposure to opportunities and a chance to sample new and exciting career fields.

Comprehensive exercises

Task 1 Fill in the blanks with the words or expressions from Readings A and B according to the meanings in the right column. The first letter of each word is already given to help your spelling. Then compare your answers with your partner.

r_____	following a pattern, especially with the same time and space between each thing and the next
a_____	to accept something to be true without question or proof
i_____	to be able to say who or what somebody/something is
s_____	to pay to receive a newspaper or magazine regularly or to use a phone line or internet service
s_____	to check something to see if it is suitable or if you want it
i_____	to buy property, shares in a company, etc. in the hope of making a profit
c_____	to arrange things or people in groups according to features that they have in common
v_____ _____	to compete for
p_____ _____	before a particular time or event
s_____ _____	to offer a particular product or service more than any other

Task 2
Complete the following sentences with the words and expressions from Task 1. Change the form if necessary.

1. If you want to learn another foreign language, you should follow the natural learning order of listening _____ speaking.
2. Instead of saving money for the future, Mr. Johnson _____ all of his earnings in collecting stamps.
3. As one of the most famous Cantonese restaurants in this area, it _____ seafood.
4. After we got off the plane, the first thing we had to do was to _____ our suitcases.
5. Though we are in great need of a marketing manager, we have to _____ all the candidates to see who the most suitable one is.
6. Mark is really a tennis fan, and so far he has spent a large sum of money _____ to several channels on tennis.
7. My old father keeps the habit of reading newspapers every day, and he reads the _____ ads most carefully to kill time.
8. Generally speaking, people who engage in _____ exercise are much healthier than those who always sit in offices.
9. To our great joy, Beijing was chosen out of many cities around the world _____ host of the 2008 Olympic Games.
10. To be honest, I _____ that you knew each other because you graduated from the same school in the same year.

Task 3
Complete the following sentences with the appropriate forms of the words given in the brackets.

1. It is very common for college students that _____ (intern) will lead to full-time employment in some cases.
2. The locals regularly shop at the supermarket to buy food, drinks, medicine and other daily _____ (necessary).
3. This area is very rich in natural resources, and it is the very reason that attracts more and more foreign _____ (invest).
4. Their research and development depends heavily on _____ (sponsor) of several hi-tech companies.
5. It's required that passengers have to pay _____ (add) charges for their extra luggage.
6. Having little work experience, he could only apply for _____ (enter) level positions at present.
7. The books in the library are _____ (class) according to subject, which makes it easier to search for the collection on a particular subject.
8. It's been believed for centuries that great leaders are _____ (essential) quite different from ordinary people.
9. This factory _____ (special) in the production of bicycles.
10. I am definitely sure few people think political _____ (active) can settle the problem of economic development.

Task 4 Rewrite the following sentences according to the examples.

Example 1: Typically, *if the pay is higher, then the internship will become more competitive.*
→ Typically, *the higher the pay, the more competitive the internship becomes.*

1. As he gets older, he becomes wiser.

2. When I know more about him, I like him more.

3. If you start earlier, you will get there sooner.

4. If there is more haste, there will be less speed.

5. If you work harder, you will make greater progress.

Example 2: Be prepared to give a 60-second introduction that describes how you can be *valuable* to an employer.
→ Be prepared to give a 60-second introduction that describes how you can be *of value* to an employer.

1. Tom is as old as Jerry and both share many interests.

2. It's always a pleasure for us to be helpful to our friends.

3. French wine is good in quality and sold all over the world.

4. To a country with a large population like China, agriculture is very important to the development of economy.

5. You can contact professionals within organizations in which you are interested and enquire about internships.

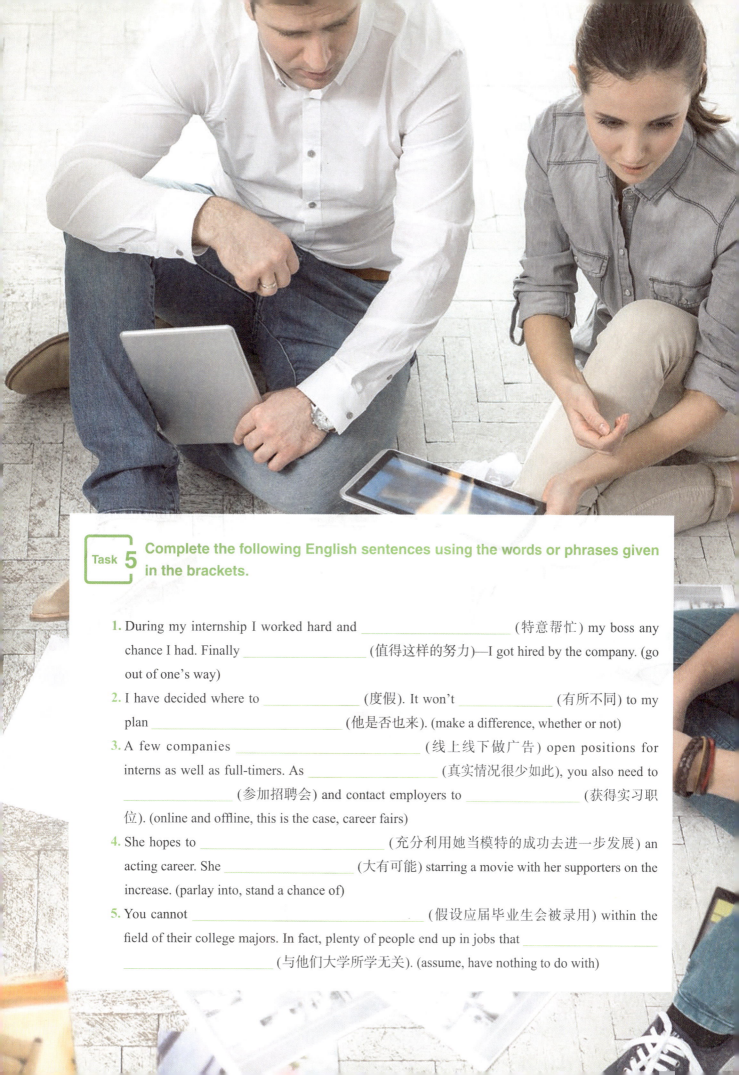

Task 5 Complete the following English sentences using the words or phrases given in the brackets.

1. During my internship I worked hard and _____ (特意帮忙) my boss any chance I had. Finally _____ (值得这样的努力)—I got hired by the company. (go out of one's way)

2. I have decided where to _____ (度假). It won't _____ (有所不同) to my plan _____ (他是否也来). (make a difference, whether or not)

3. A few companies _____ (线上线下做广告) open positions for interns as well as full-timers. As _____ (真实情况很少如此), you also need to _____ (参加招聘会) and contact employers to _____ (获得实习职位). (online and offline, this is the case, career fairs)

4. She hopes to _____ (充分利用她当模特的成功去进一步发展) an acting career. She _____ (大有可能) starring a movie with her supporters on the increase. (parlay into, stand a chance of)

5. You cannot _____ (假设应届毕业生会被录用) within the field of their college majors. In fact, plenty of people end up in jobs that _____ _____ (与他们大学所学无关). (assume, have nothing to do with)

Applied writing

职位描述

职位描述也叫职位界定,是对经过职位分析得到的关于某一具体职位的职责和工作内容进行的一种书面记录,其成果叫工作说明书。阅读下面一则职位描述,了解职位描述的写作特点。

Sample

Position:

Administrative assistant

Requirements:

Bachelor's Degree in English Business Administration major or equivalent;

Minimum of three years' related working experience;

Bilingual, with professional secretarial skills.

Major Responsibilities:

Serve as a travel coordinator for all staff;

Provide assistance with special projects and assignments as directed by the manager;

Assist the manger to prepare PowerPoint documents;

Assist Sales Department to maintain promotion materials and files.

Contact:

All the résumés should be sent to Human Resource Department within two weeks.

Email: LightNobel@hotmail.com

Writing task

After four months' internship as an Administrative assistant, Li Ming is asked to fill in the form about his job description.

You are required to help him finish the following form according to the Chinese information given below.

职位：

行政助理

岗位职责：

1. 协助行政总监完成公司行政事务管理。
2. 协助日常行政工作的组织与管理。
3. 各种规章制度监督与执行。
4. 协助行政总监招聘、培训等工作。
5. 会务安排，做好会前准备、会议记录和会后资料整理工作。

岗位要求：

1. 相关专业大专及以上学历，2年以上工作经验，有服务性企业工作经验者优先。
2. 熟练操作Word、Excel、PowerPoint等办公软件。
3. 具有较强的时间管理潜力及解决突发事件潜力。

Internship

Name: _____

Position: _____

Responsibilities:

1. _____
2. _____
3. _____
4. _____
5. _____

Requirements:

1. _____
2. _____
3. _____

Project performing

💬 Guidelines

This project aims to simulate relevant situations of conducting internship. The whole task is divided into three steps. Step one is about trying to find out different types of internship. Step two focuses on how to apply for an internship. Step three is concerned with writing a job description.

Please follow the task description to complete the project.

Task description

Step one

- Organize a small group of 4 to 6 students in your class;
- Brainstorm and share different types of internship;
- Give a presentation to introduce the type of internship that you prefer.

Step two

- List as many ways as possible that you can apply for an internship;
- Divide the group into two sides: One side is fresh graduates, the other is career counselors;
- Take turns to play roles: The side of fresh graduates asks for advice on how to apply for internships, and the other side gives practical advice.

Step three

- The side of fresh graduates asks for requirements for and responsibilities of a certain internship, and the side of career counselors tells them about the job description accordingly;
- Discuss the job description with group members;
- Give a presentation to the whole class about your understanding of it.

Grammar

完成时态的基本用法和特殊用法

1. 现在完成时

基本用法/特殊用法	例句
表示从过去开始并持续到现在（也许还会持续下去）的动作或状态，常和for, since 引导的状语或与how long连用	He has lived here for over ten years. We've been good friends since we were children. How long have you known her?
表示某件事发生在过去，但这事往往和现在有关系和影响	Your nose is bleeding. Has anybody hit you? I have washed my car. It is very clean.
常和表示"直到现在"的状语连用，如before (now), It's the first/second time…, so far, up till now, up to the present, ever, never等	He hasn't appeared on TV before now. She has never eaten a mango before. It's the first time I have seen a pagoda. This is the best tea I have ever drunk.
表示最近发生的动作，常和just, yet, already, recently, still等副词连用	The rain has already stopped. Have you seen Lewis recently? He still hasn't finished his work.

2. 过去完成时

基本用法/特殊用法	例句
表示过去的某件事发生在另一件过去的事之前（过去的过去）	When I arrived, Jane had just left. Up till then we had only covered half the distance.
常用于宾语从句（间接引语）、状语从句和定语从句中	He said he had been in China for over ten years. I didn't begin the work until he had gone. She wore the necklace her mother had left her.
用于hope, intend, mean, think等动词表示未实现的愿望	I had hoped to be back last night, but I didn't catch the train. We had thought to return early but they wouldn't let us go.

3. 将来完成时

基本用法/特殊用法	例句
表示将来某时某动作已完成或某事情已发生	Tom will have had his exams by 18 December. By this summer we'll have been here for five years.
常与by, not… till/until+时间连用；还常与build, complete, finish等表示完成意义的动词连用	I will have retired by the year 2035. I hope I will have finished this report by the end of the day.

Task 1 Complete the following sentences using proper forms of the given verbs.

1. Up to now I _____ (visit) twenty countries.
2. He _____ (type) six letters so far.
3. They _____ (never quarrel) like this before.
4. We _____ (not be) there since we were young.
5. She _____ (drive) the same car for fifteen years.
6. By the time we arrived, the party _____ (finish).
7. After we _____ (discuss) it on the phone, I wrote him a letter about it.
8. Before we took Tim to the theatre, he _____ (never see) a stage play before.
9. They _____ (complete) the new bridge by the end of the year.
10. Our country _____ (become) a powerful one by the middle of the 21st century.

Task 2 Choose the best answer to complete each of the following sentences.

1. —_____ you _____ the gas off?
   —I don't like it to be on when I'm not at home.
   A. Had; turned   B. Have; turned   C. Are; turning   D. Do; turn

2. We _____ to the tennis club since we moved here.
   A. have belonged   B. belong   C. belonged   D. are belonging

3. When I went into the bathroom, I found that the bath _____.
   A. overflows   B. overflowed   C. had overflowed   D. is overflowing

4. I was sure that I _____ him before.
   A. had met   B. am meeting   C. meet   D. met

5. When I saw the vase in the shop window, I knew it was exactly what I _____.
   A. looked for   B. is looking for   C. had been looking for   D. have looked for

6. She learned that scientists _____ a breakthrough in the treatment of that disease.
   A. have made   B. had made   C. made   D. will have made

7. It was the first time I _____ in a foreign country.
   A. have been   B. was   C. had been   D. am

8. Jane _____ me up three times this morning already.
   A. rang   B. is ringing   C. had rung   D. has rung

9. By the time you get home, I _____ the house from top to bottom.
   A. have cleaned   B. will clean   C. will have cleaned   D. am cleaning

10. They _____ the work on the great dam by the end of this decade.
    A. will have completed   B. have completed
    C. complete   D. had completed

Task 3 Translate the following sentences into English.

1. 我还没来得及阻拦，她已冲出门去了。
2. 我本想这个周末去看望他的，但没去成。
3. 到现在为止，这工作还算容易。
4. 他从小就戴眼镜。
5. 到年底时你们将完成所有的课程。

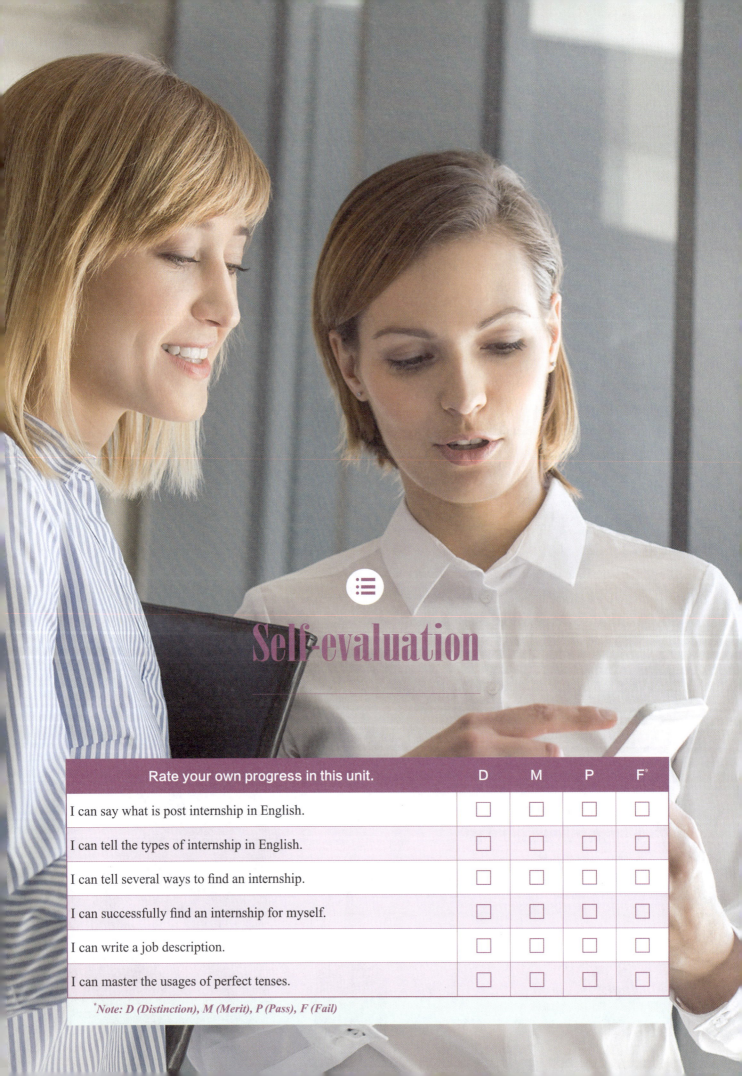

Self-evaluation

Rate your own progress in this unit.	D	M	P	F*
I can say what is post internship in English.	☐	☐	☐	☐
I can tell the types of internship in English.	☐	☐	☐	☐
I can tell several ways to find an internship.	☐	☐	☐	☐
I can successfully find an internship for myself.	☐	☐	☐	☐
I can write a job description.	☐	☐	☐	☐
I can master the usages of perfect tenses.	☐	☐	☐	☐

*Note: D (Distinction), M (Merit), P (Pass), F (Fail)

Culture

实习，顾名思义，是在实践中学习。在经过一段时间的学习之后，或者说当学习告一段落的时候，我们需要了解自己所学知识应当如何应用在实践中。因为任何知识都源于实践、归于实践，所以要付诸实践来检验所学。实习一般包括大学里的学生实习和公司里的员工实习。

大学生实习，是指在校大学生进入政府机关、企事业单位和社会团体等用人单位进行教学实习、生产实习，以开展实践教学、培养学生工程与实践能力和创新精神，包括在校内校外的工程训练中心、专业实训中心、专业实训基地、实习基地、实习实训基地的各类实习。

近年来，在高校和政府机关、企事业单位和社会团体等用人单位共同努力下，产学研融合不断深入，大学生实习工作稳定开展，质量稳步提高。

Task 1 Watch the following video clip, and then complete the mind map with missing words and phrases.

Why internships are important to your career

Internships help to build your ___1___ and find your first job.

- Internships where work ___2___ comes from give a safe space to practice the skills learned from school and apply them in the real world.

- Internship is the number of ___3___ opportunities you will experience. So take the time to get to know everyone in the ___4___, not just your managers and high ups.

- By investing your time in doing internship or co-op work placement, your résumé is going to ___5___ big time.

Task 2 List the ideal companies and positions to do your internship and explain the reasons for your choice.

Unit 6
Campus Recruitment

Learning objectives

After studying this unit, you should be able to:
- get familiar with the words and expressions concerning campus recruitment;
- understand how companies conduct campus recruitment;
- know more about campus recruitment and how to get involved in it;
- be clear about how to build campus recruitment strategies;
- master the skills of writing a letter of application;
- be expert at the usages of modal verbs.

Warm-up

Task 1 Watch the video clip *Huawei 2018 campus recruitment*, which contains some famous sayings. Complete these sayings according to what you hear and try to translate them into Chinese. Some key words and phrases are listed for you.

> majority 大多数人   reflect 反思；思考
> continual 继续不断的   observatory 天文台；天文观测站

1. The _____ of life is to explore the endless things not yet known.
   —Emile Zola

2. A soul without _____ is like an observatory without the telescope.
   —Albert Einstein

3. Whenever you find yourself on the side of majority, it is time to pause and _____.
   —Mark Twain

4. Man's duty is to have the _____ to seek the truth.
   —Nicolas Copernicus

5. Young people who make big _____ are mostly those who dare to challenge the rules of law.
   —Pierre de Fermat

6. The greatest _____ for me is not the height I have reached, but the continual climb.
   —Gauss

7. Normally it is the last key on the _____ which opens the door.
   —Qian Xuesen

Task 2 Look at the poster and answer the following questions orally.

1. What company held this campus recruitment?
2. What position could be applied for?
3. What departments were in need of this position?
4. When was this campus recruitment held?

Li Ming makes use of the ways that he learns in Unit 5 and successfully finds an internship for himself, an assistant to the HR manager of a trading company. At present, Li Ming, other interns and the HR colleagues are preparing and organizing the campus recruitment for the company. To support them, the HR Department plans to give them some training. Before the training, the HR manager asks them to read the article *How companies conduct campus recruitment* as below.

Pre-reading questions

1. Have you ever taken part in any campus recruitment?
2. Do you know how to apply for a job?

How companies conduct campus recruitment

The process of hiring good candidates directly from colleges and universities is called campus recruitment. It is the process through which promising students are involved into job according to their results and merits. In this way the companies can also utilize the expertise of the students in building an effective pipeline. They target specific institutions for recruiting candidates according to their requirements.

The process of recruitment begins with gathering information before recruitment. As a recruiter, the first and the foremost thing that you need to do is set the goals for recruitment. You have to find out the areas where you need to recruit a candidate and also the qualities a candidate should possess to fulfill the needs of the organization.

As an employer you have to jot down the qualities you are looking for in a candidate to meet the expectations of your company. You have to decide the job role of the candidate and also need to be introspective while judging a candidate for a particular designation.

To make the process of applying for a job easier, a recruiter can use the various social media platforms for job advertising. Today's generation is more attached to the digital channel and so viewing a job on a Facebook page or on the YouTube can make them feel more at ease regarding the job. The youngsters are technologically inclined and hence this platform can be very well used to allure them for a job.

The JD or the job description should be spiced up with impressive words and descriptions. It should not be a monotonous one, stating a list of do's and don'ts for an applicant. If you are a manager, you should be able to explain all the criteria of the designation clearly in the job description while writing it. There should also be a separate mention regarding the salary package in the job description.

A company needs to shortlist the colleges and universities in order to conduct the campus hiring. You should know what your company is looking for in a candidate, and according to that you should choose the educational institutions having students who will be able to fulfill this criteria. You as a recruiter should be aware of the overall performance of an institution in terms of scoring and accordingly you should keep those colleges in your list from where you can pick up employees.

As recruiters you'd better not visit a college campus for conducting an interview during the end of a semester. The students remain busy with their examination at that time and cannot concentrate in the interview much. Also it is the peak time when all the companies drop in to hire candidates from the campus. As a recruiter, you need to be careful as to when to conduct the process of selection.

(484 words)

New words

*candidate	/ˈkændɪdeɪt/	n.	应试者，应聘者
▲merit	/ˈmerɪt/	n.	优点；价值；功绩
pipeline	/ˈpaɪplaɪn/	n.	管道；传递途径
*target	/ˈtɑːgɪt/	v.	瞄准；面向；对准
*institution	/ˌɪnstɪˈtjuːʃn/	n.	（大学、银行等）机构
▲foremost	/ˈfɔːməʊst/	a.	最重要的；最前的
*possess	/pəˈzes/	v.	拥有，持有
▲fulfill	/fʊlˈfɪl/	v.	履行；实现；满足
jot	/dʒɒt/	v.	匆忙记下；略记；摘要；记载下来
introspective	/ˌɪntrəˈspektɪv/	a.	内省的；反省的
designation	/ˌdezɪɡˈneɪʃn/	n.	委任；选派
*platform	/ˈplætfɔːm/	n.	平台；站台；月台
*ease	/iːz/	n.	自在；无忧无虑
▲regarding	/rɪˈɡɑːdɪŋ/	prep.	关于；至于

technologically	/ˌteknəˈlɒdʒɪkəli/	ad.	技术上地
*incline	/ɪnˈklaɪn, ˈɪnklaɪn/	v.	（使）倾向于；有……的趋势；（使）倾斜
*hence	/hens/	ad.	因此；由此
▲allure	/əˈlʊə(r)/	v.	吸引；引诱
▲spice	/spaɪs/	v.	在……中加香料；给……增添趣味；使……变得刺激
▲impressive	/ɪmˈpresɪv/	a.	给人留下深刻印象的；令人赞叹的
▲monotonous	/məˈnɒtənəs/	a.	单调的；乏味的
▲criteria	/kraɪˈtɪəriə/	n.	标准（criterion 的复数）
*aware	/əˈweə(r)/	a.	意识到的；明白的；有……意识的
▲overall	/ˌəʊvərˈɔːl/	a.	全面的；综合的；总体的
shortlist	/ˈʃɔːtlɪst/	v.	把……列入入围名单
scoring	/ˈskɔːrɪŋ/	n.	得分
▲accordingly	/əˈkɔːdɪŋli/	ad.	因此，于是；相应地
*concentrate	/ˈkɒnsntreɪt/	v.	专注；专心致志
▲peak	/piːk/	n.	山峰；最高点；顶点

🗨 Phrases & expressions

fulfill the needs of	满足……的需求
jot down	匆匆记下
meet the expectations of	满足……的期望
feel at ease	释然；心里踏实；舒气
be inclined to do something	倾向于做……
spice up	增加香料，增添趣味
be aware of	知道；意识到
in terms of	在……方面；依据……
drop in	顺道拜访；突然拜访
campus recruitment	校园招聘
the first and the foremost thing	第一要务
social media platforms	社交媒体平台
digital channel	数字频道
job description (JD)	工作职责说明
do's and don'ts	应该做什么及不应该做什么
salary package	薪资福利；薪酬
educational institutions	教育机构
peak time	峰值时间

Proper names

Facebook　　脸书；脸谱网（创立于2004年2月4日，总部位于美国加利福尼亚州门洛帕克）

YouTube　　油管视频网站（一家专供用户免费上传、观赏、分享视频的共享网站，创立于2005年2月15日，后被谷歌公司收购）

生词数	生词率	*B级词汇	*A级词汇	▲四、六级词汇	超纲词汇
30	6.20%	5	5	12	8

Notes

1. **campus recruitment**

   Campus recruitment refers to the process whereby employers undertake an organized program of attracting and hiring students who are about to graduate from schools, colleges, and universities. Campus recruitment programs are widespread in most of the world. Employers commonly attend campuses to promote employment vacancies and career opportunities to students who are considering their options following graduation. Selection methods used by employers include interviews, aptitude tests, role plays, written assessments, group discussions and presentations.

2. **salary package**

   Salary packages typically include your base salary as well as additional benefits, incentives or rewards, such as superannuation, annual and sick leave, car allowance or bonuses. With a salary package, money is usually deducted from your salary before tax for these items or services.

After-reading tasks

Task 1 Read the passage and fill in the blanks with appropriate information from the passage.

　　The process of recruitment begins with gathering ___1___ before recruitment. As a recruiter, the first thing that you need to do is set the ___2___ for recruitment. You have to find out the areas where you need to recruit a candidate and also the ___3___ a candidate should possess to fulfill the needs of the organization. To make the process of applying for a job easier, a recruiter can use the various ___4___ platforms for job advertising. Today's generation is more attached to the ___5___ and so viewing a job on a Facebook page or on the YouTube can make them feel more at ease regarding the job.

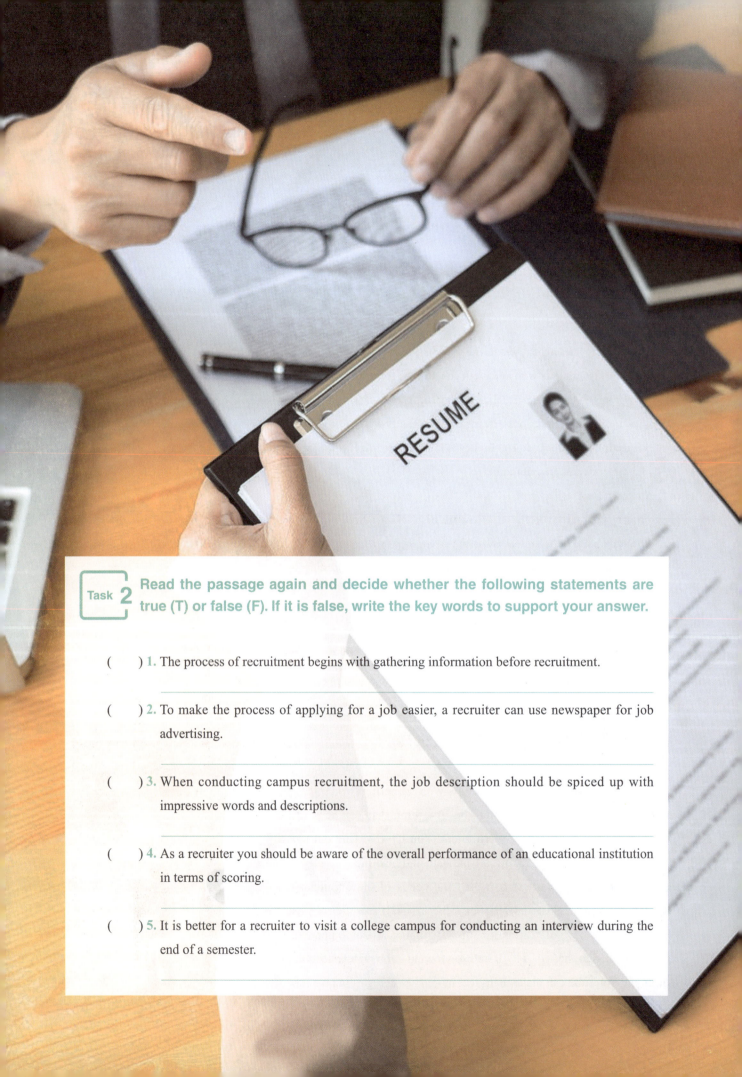

Task 2 Read the passage again and decide whether the following statements are true (T) or false (F). If it is false, write the key words to support your answer.

(　　) 1. The process of recruitment begins with gathering information before recruitment.

_____

(　　) 2. To make the process of applying for a job easier, a recruiter can use newspaper for job advertising.

_____

(　　) 3. When conducting campus recruitment, the job description should be spiced up with impressive words and descriptions.

_____

(　　) 4. As a recruiter you should be aware of the overall performance of an educational institution in terms of scoring.

_____

(　　) 5. It is better for a recruiter to visit a college campus for conducting an interview during the end of a semester.

_____

Listening and speaking

Task 1 After reading the article *How companies conduct campus recruitment,* Li Ming has a question: Why do companies conduct campus recruitment? During a tea break, Li Ming talks about it with Mr. Wei, the HR manager. Listen to Mr. Wei's response on "the advantages of campus recruitment" three times and complete the following note.

Campus recruitment offers	• _____ advantages to both the companies and the job _____.
It is possible for companies to	• _____ best and quality candidates for different job posts with a _____ time.
Campus recruitment helps in	• _____ time and efforts of the companies.
This is useful in reduced	• _____ effort and time as well.
A company through effective campus recruitment	• finds an opportunity to establish a _____ with _____ graduates each year.
Fresh and talented graduates will work more	• _____ with their first company. Hence, this will increase the _____ loyalty among applicants.

Task 2 When reading the article *How companies conduct campus recruitment*, Li Ming also notices that "recruiter" is mentioned several times. He is curious to know how the company defines the job position of "campus recruiter" and what a campus recruiter does exactly, so he talks to Mr. Wei again. Listen to their conversation three times and choose the best answers to complete the following sentences.

1. A campus recruiter is often devoted _____ to finding and hiring college students for internships or entry-level positions.
   A. full-time   B. part-time   C. voluntarily   D. much time
2. The training on _____ is coming very soon for interns.
   A. technology   B. strategy   C. marketing   D. relationship building
3. A campus recruiter needs to develop _____.
   A. an internship plan   B. a career plan
   C. a marketing plan   D. a campus recruitment plan
4. A campus recruiter needs to build relationships with _____ in order to promote the company.
   A. campus career services staff   B. campus IT services staff
   C. campus student services staff   D. campus library services staff
5. Campus recruiters are also the _____ of recruiting events or career fairs.
   A. advisers   B. leaders   C. organizers   D. supporters

Task 3 In order to learn more about campus recruitment, Li Ming talks to an experienced HR colleague, Mr. Wen, to find out the common practices for campus recruiting. Listen to their conversation three times and fill in the blanks.

Li Ming: Hello, Mr. Wen. How many times have you participated in our company's campus recruitment?

Mr. Wen: Three times. It is always the big ___1___ in the HR department.

Li Ming: As an intern, I need your help with a few questions on campus recruitment.

Mr. Wen: Sure. No problem.

Li Ming: Who is involved with campus recruiting?

Mr. Wen: Employers, campus recruiters, college campus career services staff and college students are the main ___2___. Other key roles can be the hiring managers and the employees from other company ___3___ like IT, marketing, law and more.

Li Ming: What is the first thing that a recruiter needs to do?

Mr. Wen: Decide the company's ___4___ for hiring. For example, ask some basic questions like: Are you searching for some skills, such as computer programming or ___5___ analysis? Are you recruiting for your head office, or other offices?

Li Ming:	I see. How do you usually build a campus recruiting team?
Mr. Wen:	By answering such basic questions as mentioned above, we can decide which employees and ___6___ need to be on the team. Then we create a plan to solve how the team will be ___7___.
Li Ming:	How do you attract a new ___8___ of students?
Mr. Wen:	We use the ___9___ social media platforms for job advertising. We also build and manage talent ___10___ and keep communications through social media.
Li Ming:	Mr. Wen, thank you so much indeed. Are you one of the trainers for the coming training arranged for us interns?
Mr. Wen:	Yes. I will work together with the HR manager Mr. Wei to train all the interns.
Li Ming:	Glad to hear that. Look forward to seeing you soon.

Task 4

In a training class, the HR manager Mr. Wei gives all the interns a lecture on developing college recruitment strategies. In the beginning, he requires them to read an article *How to build a high-impact campus recruitment strategy* after the training. He also requires each intern to do a follow-up presentation on this article in the next class. Listen to the part of his lecture three times and tick off the items mentioned.

☐ 1. a talent community   ☐ 2. candidate sourcing

☐ 3. source young talent   ☐ 4. candidate interview

☐ 5. entry-level employees   ☐ 6. experienced employees

☐ 7. connect on campus   ☐ 8. stay in touch throughout the year

☐ 9. build a strong connection ☐ 10. build a strong employer brand

Task 5

Li Ming feels excited to work as an intern to participate in his company's campus recruitment. He can't help sharing this experience with his father. Work in pairs. Make up a dialogue between Li Ming and his father, including the details on what Li Ming has done in his company's campus recruitment. Role-play the dialogue in class.

Task 6

Li Ming and other interns are required to give a short speech on how to conduct a successful campus recruiting event in their training class. Suppose you are Li Ming and give the short speech in class.

After the training, Li Ming follows the instruction of the HR manager to study the article *How to build a high-impact campus recruitment strategy* as below. He needs to learn more skills to get himself ready for the coming task.

How to build a high-impact campus recruitment strategy

With summer in full swing and the fall semester just a couple of months away, many companies are starting to think about their campus recruitment efforts. And for good reason—college recruiting can be a great way to find your best hires and keep recruitment costs at bay. Here are some important things to keep in mind as you get started.

Choose your schools carefully

Before you begin developing your strategy, it's important to identify the schools that are most likely to provide you with valuable candidates. Depending on your budget, start by creating a list of 5 to 10 schools that offer some of the key majors you're targeting. Then, divide that list into two tiers. The first tier should be your primary schools—the ones where you think you're most likely to find your top talent—while the second tier can consist of "dream schools" and schools that are outside of your geographical area. Once you've identified your target schools, you can start creating your strategy.

Develop ongoing relationships

Like other types of recruitment, campus recruiting is built on strong relationships, so getting to know the career centers at top schools is extremely important when you're starting out. Reaching out to career counselors and telling them a little bit about your company and what types of candidates you're looking for can make a big difference when it comes to getting the right hires. In addition to being able to provide you with relevant candidates, the staff at the career services centers can act as the perfect bridge between your team and various university departments.

Have a consistent campus presence

An ongoing presence on campus is a great way to build a strong employer brand, and it can make a big difference when it comes to attracting the right talent. Attending regular career fairs and campus events is a good way to establish this type of presence, but you shouldn't stop there. Creating a brand ambassador program to help students understand and connect with your brand is an effective way to grow your presence and potentially increase your reach. And because it can offer students insights into your products and company culture, this type of program can be a wonderful way to build an impression that can have a long-lasting impact down the line.

Build an ongoing pipeline

Depending on your hiring needs, your impulse may be to target only upperclassmen who are looking for internships and entry-level jobs. But developing a more robust strategy could actually be beneficial in the long run. Taking the time to connect with first- and second-year students at career fairs and developing a database of potential candidates can significantly improve your recruiting efforts and hiring time as students get closer to graduation.

(486 words)

New words

▲impact	/ˈɪmpækt/	n.	巨大影响；撞击
*swing	/swɪŋ/	n.	行程；秋千
*bay	/beɪ/	n.	海湾；湖湾
*budget	/ˈbʌdʒɪt/	n.	预算，预算费
tier	/tɪə(r)/	n.	层；等级
*talent	/ˈtælənt/	n.	人才；有能力的人；天资
▲ongoing	/ˈɒŋɡəʊɪŋ/	a.	仍在进行的；不断前进的
▲consistent	/kənˈsɪstənt/	a.	始终如一的，一致的；坚持的
*presence	/ˈprezns/	n.	出席；在场；（某物的）存在
*brand	/brænd/	n.	商标；（商品的）品牌
*ambassador	/æmˈbæsədə(r)/	n.	大使
*potentially	/pəˈtenʃəli/	ad.	可能地；潜在地
*insight	/ˈɪnsaɪt/	n.	洞察力；观点
*impression	/ɪmˈpreʃn/	n.	印象，感想；印记，压痕
*long-lasting	/ˌlɒŋ ˈlɑːstɪŋ/	a.	持久的；长期的
▲impulse	/ˈɪmpʌls/	n.	推动力；脉冲；冲击
upperclassmen	/ˌʌpəˈklɑːsmen/	n.	美国高年级学生
▲robust	/rəʊˈbʌst/	a.	强健的；健康的
▲database	/ˈdeɪtəbeɪs/	n.	数据库，资料库
*significantly	/sɪɡˈnɪfɪkəntli/	ad.	显著地；相当数量地

Phrases & expressions

in full swing	在热烈进行中;处于兴盛阶段
a couple of something	几个人;几件事物
keep... at bay	控制……
consist of	由……构成
reach out	伸手去取
have a long-lasting impact	对……产生持久的影响
down the line	在某一时刻;在某一环节
in the long run	长远,终究
campus recruitment strategy	校园招聘策略
fall semester	秋季学期;秋季班
top schools	顶尖大学
career fair	招聘会
campus events	校园活动
brand ambassador program	品牌大使计划

生词数	生词率	*B级词汇	*A级词汇	▲四、六级词汇	超纲词汇
21	4.32%	6	7	6	2

After-reading tasks

Task 1 Match each practice in the right column with the corresponding campus recruitment strategy in the left column.

(   ) 1. Choose your schools carefully   A. Creating a brand ambassador program

(   ) 2. Develop ongoing relationships   B. Taking the time to connect with first- and second-year students at career fairs

(   ) 3. Have a consistent campus presence   C. Dividing that list of schools into two tiers

(   ) 4. Build an ongoing pipeline   D. Getting to know the career centers at top schools

Unit 6 | Campus Recruitment

Task 2 Translate the following paragraph into Chinese.

Like other types of recruitment, campus recruiting is built on strong relationships so getting to know the career centers at top schools is extremely important when you're starting out. Reaching out to career counselors and telling them a little bit about your company and what types of candidates you're looking for can make a big difference when it comes to getting the right hires. In addition to being able to provide you with relevant candidates, the staff at the career services centers can act as the perfect bridge between your team and various university departments.

Comprehensive exercises

Task 1 Fill in the blanks with the words or expressions from Readings A and B according to the meanings in the right column. The first letter of each word is already given to help your spelling. Then compare your answers with your partner.

f_____	to perform or carry out an order, duty, promise, etc.
t_____	to direct advertising, criticism, or a product at someone
a_____	to have a very powerful attraction
e_____	to create or set something in a particular way
c_____	to give all of your attention to one particular activity, subject, or problem
i_____	causing admiration by giving one a feeling of size, importance, quality, etc.
c_____	to be made of or formed from something
s_____	to add excitement or interest to something
j_____	to write something quickly on a piece of paper so that you remember it
d_____	to come for a visit, esp. without having received an invitation for a specific time

Task 2 Complete the following sentences with the words and expressions from Task 1. Change the form if necessary.

1. Now that you have graduated, it's the time to _____ your life with a career you'll enjoy!
2. Vocational colleges should _____ close contact with business organizations for cooperation and development.
3. Let me _____ your telephone number so that I can call you later.
4. During four months' internship in this supermarket, Mary carefully _____ her role and done her duty perfectly.
5. We all admitted that he had delivered a very _____ speech on how to master a foreign language in half a year.
6. The beautiful beaches of Hainan _____ many tourists from the mainland of China.
7. It's a simple dish to prepare, mainly _____ rice and vegetables.
8. The company is selling off its restaurant chain to _____ on its main business of real estate.
9. The advertisement for the energy drink is _____ specifically at young people.
10. Welcome to _____ for a chat whenever you're in the neighborhood.

Task 3 Complete the following sentences with the appropriate forms of the words given in the brackets.

1. Language cannot be separated from cultural reality: it is lived _____ (present) of culture, making human activity meaningful.
2. Whether or not a drug is _____ (effect) depends on many factors, including how consistently the patient follows the instructions for taking it.
3. For candidates, the _____ (recruit) may be the best person to ask questions regarding opportunities of personal development.
4. The workforce have recently been calling for their working hours to be reduced. Many companies have _____ (according) switched to a five-day week.
5. Considering his knee injury there can be little _____ (expect) of him winning the competition.
6. Electronic files, although _____ (technology) advanced, cannot replace paper files in many cases.
7. This smart phone is popular for its good design and _____ (easy) of use.
8. The company's fastest growing _____ (geography) market was in Asia, which increased by 22%.
9. On paper our profits look very _____ (impress), but in reality we made very little money last year.
10. After a few job interviews, Jimmy found a good degree was a basic _____ (require) for most jobs.

Unit 6 | Campus Recruitment

Task 4 Rewrite the following sentences according to the examples.

Example 1: As a recruiter, *what you need to do first and foremost* is set the goals for recruitment.
→ As a recruiter, *the first and the foremost thing that you need to do* is set the goals for recruitment.

1. He is now in love and not what he used to be.

2. What is happening outside has nothing to do with us.

3. What I'm going to do first when I get home is have a good sleep.

4. The pictures reminded her of what she had ever experienced in that summer internship.

5. As an employer you have to jot down what you are looking for in a candidate to meet the expectations of your company.

Example 2: *You can build a strong employer brand well by way of* an ongoing presence on campus.
→ An ongoing presence on campus is *a great way to build a strong employer brand*.

1. You can possibly protect environment by way of bicycling.

2. You can keep good health effectively by way of appropriate exercise.

3. You can find your best hires and keep recruitment costs at bay successfully by way of college recruiting.

4. Among the young people of his age, he is different by way of his humorous and witty conversations.

5. Today's generation is more attached to the digital channel and so the employers can increase their reach wonderfully by way of job advertising on social networks.

Task 5 — Complete the following English sentences using the words or phrases given in the brackets.

1. All successful business people do not _____ (在很年轻时就起步), but _____ (他们都具有的品质之一) is their _____ (为目标而长期坚持不懈的努力). (start out, possess, in the long run)

2. _____ (社交媒体平台也许是一个极佳渠道) for job advertising _____ (就用户数量众多而言). And you can _____ (通过添加图片而使招聘广告更令人感兴趣) along with the job descriptions. (in terms of, spice up)

3. It's wise for the company _____ (以潜在市场为目标) of young people by _____ (制订品牌大使计划), which _____ (提供对公司文化的深入了解) as well as its products. (target, create a program, an insight into)

4. _____ (通过参与社区服务) Li Ming as a freshman _____ (更加融入了校园生活) and he also _____ (向学长们学习) more experience _____ (以达到大学的要求). (get involved in, attached to, upperclassman, meet the requirements)

5. The Internet _____ (极大地影响了人们的生活方式). More and more electronic products and Apps have been developed _____ (以满足人们的各种需求), and meanwhile _____ (使发生了很大变化) in many ways, such as reading habits and sports events. (make an impact on, fulfil a need, make a big difference)

Applied writing

简历

简历是对个人学历、工作经历、特长、爱好及其他有关情况所做的简明扼要的书面描述,是有针对性的自我介绍的一种规范化、逻辑化的书面表达。阅读下面一则个人简历,了解其写作特点。

Sample

Name	Zhang Li	Gender	Female
Age	22	Tel.	020-33445588
Job objective	Sales rep.		
Address	602, Building 3, Great Street, Guangzhou, 510032, China		
Education	Sept. 2018–July 2021: School of Adult Education, Guangdong Light Industry Polytechnic		
	Sept. 2015–July 2018: No. 1 Middle School in Guangzhou		
Foreign languages	Excellent English, fair Japanese		
Work experiences	Jan. 2021–June 2021 internship: worked as a salesperson in ABC company July 2020–Aug. 2020 part-time-job: worked as a sales rep. in Changcheng Company July 2019–Aug. 2019 part-time-job: worked as a receptionist at Garden Hotel		
Certificates	Certificate of CET6, Driver's License		
Social activities	Sept. 2019 –July 2020: Head of the Students' Union		
Hobbies	Reading, listening to music, traveling, playing basketball		
References	To be sent upon request		

Writing task

Li Ming is a job hunter and he is going to write a résumé. You are required to help him finish the form according to the Chinese information given below.

李明，男，23岁，家住中国广州市花园路2栋1302号
邮政编码：510022
电话：159*****899
申请职位：电脑编程员
教育：
2018年9月—2021年7月　就读于广东轻工职业技术学院计算机学院
2015年9月—2018年7月　就读于广州第八中学
语言程度：精通英语和粤语
工作经历：
2021年1月—2021年6月　在广州长盛公司实习，担任电脑编程员
2020年7月—2020年8月　在惠州长远软件公司兼职做程序员
2019年7月—2019年8月　在广州启航电脑公司兼职电脑维护员
证书：大学英语四级证书，全国计算机等级考试三级证书
社会活动：计算机协会
爱好：旅行、踢足球、听音乐
推荐信：如需要，随时呈交

Name		Gender	
Age		Tel.	
Job objective			
Address			
Education			
Languages			
Work experiences			
Certificates			
Social activities			
Hobbies			
References			

Project performing

💬 Guidelines

This project aims to simulate relevant situations of writing an application letter. The whole task is divided into three steps. Step one is about trying to find out the functions of an application letter. Step two focuses on the actual content in the letter. Step three is concerned with writing an application letter.

Please follow the task description to complete the project.

Task description

Step one

- Organize a small group of 4 to 6 students in your class;
- Brainstorm and share the functions and importance of an application letter;
- Give a presentation to introduce the effect of an application letter on finding a job.

Step two

- List as much content as possible that you can use to write an application letter;
- Divide the group into two sides: One side is counselors, the other is job seekers;
- Take turns to play roles: The side of counselors demonstrates how to write an application letter effectively, and the other side follows them carefully.

Step three

- The side of counselors asks for opinions about an application letter, and the side of job seekers writes an application letter accordingly;
- Discuss the application letter with group members;
- Give a presentation to the whole class about your application letter.

Grammar

情态动词的基本用法和特殊用法

情态动词	基本用法/特殊用法	例句
can	表示能力，现在或将来的情况	She can run very fast. Who can answer this question?
	表示许可，允许做某事，意思接近may	You can take the book home. You can park here.
	用于否定句，表示否定的推测	That can't be Mary. She is in hospital.
could	can的过去式，表示过去的情况，表示能力或可能性	I could drive a car before I left school. She couldn't answer the teacher's questions. He could be pretty naughty when he was a child.
	表示委婉地提出请求、想法、建议等	Could you send me an application form? Could you show me the way?
	用于虚拟条件句	You could get into university if you applied.
	could have done 表示"那时可能"或表示"本来可以""差点就"	Don't worry. They could have just forgotten to phone. He could have sent a message.
may	表示"可以""可能"	You may only borrow books for two weeks. Anna may know Tom's address.
	表示祝愿	May you be happy!
might	may的过去式，表示过去的情况，表示"可以""可能"	He asked if he might use the phone. He said he might be late.
	用于虚拟条件句	If you invited him, he might come.
must	表示"必须""一定要"；否定形式表示"不得""一定不要"	I must remember to go to the bank today. You mustn't take photos here. It's forbidden.
	表示推想；must have done 表示对过去的肯定推测	You must be hungry. Have something to eat. We must have read the same report.
ought to	表示"应该""应当"，意思接近should	I ought to write to him today. You ought to read this book. It's marvelous.

情态动词	基本用法/特殊用法	例句
need	用于否定结构，表示"不必"	You needn't make two copies. One will do. You needn't come to the meeting if you're too busy.
	可作为及物动词，表示"需要"，后面跟名词、代词或不定式	I need a new film for my camera. The instrument needed to be sterilized.
dare	表示"敢"，过去式dared	She dare not say what she thinks. No one dared speak of it.
	可作为及物动词，后面跟名词、代词或不定式	He will dare any danger. He dares to accuse the boss of dishonesty.

Task 1 Choose the best answer to complete each of the following sentences.

1. —I am seeing Dr Evans next week.
   —That _____ be right. He is on holiday then.
   A. mustn't   B. can't   C. hasn't to   D. hasn't got to

2. It's the third time she's been skating this week. She _____ really enjoy it.
   A. must   B. should   C. ought to   D. had better

3. I promised to get there before 5 o'clock, but now the rain is pouring down. They _____ for me impatiently.
   A. may wait   B. ought to wait   C. could wait   D. must be waiting

4. Our house is on the top of the hill, so in summer the wind _____ be pretty cold.
   A. must   B. can   C. ought to   D. need

5. Sir, you _____ hunt deer here, for they are preserved by the government.
   A. oughtn't to   B. can't   C. won't   D. needn't

6. You _____ phone him if you want to, but you _____. He is sure to phone you.
   A. may; mustn't   B. have to; needn't   C. can; doesn't need   D. can; needn't

7. He _____ full marks, but he was so careless as to make a spelling mistake.
   A. must have gained   B. can have gained   C. could have gained   D. must gain

8. —Where _____ Mary have put the empty bottles?
   —She _____ them away. They must be somewhere.
   A. can; can't have thrown   B. must; needn't
   C. must; must have thrown   D. can't; must throw

9. —Mum, I climbed to get the Teddy Bear from the top of the shelf.
   —My goodness! You _____ yourself. You _____ do that next time.
   A. must have hurt; mustn't   B. should have hurt; can't
   C. may have hurt; mustn't   D. might have hurt; won't be able to

10. Hurry up. The class _____. I'll be late again.
    A. must begin   B. may begin   C. should have begun   D. must have begun

Task 2 Please underline the correct modal verbs. You may choose more than one answer.

1. You *can/may* take the book home.
2. Even if he had been there, he *couldn't/can't* have helped you.
3. *May/Might* I have a little brandy?
4. You *needn't/don't need to* walk. I'll give you a lift.
5. The garden *doesn't need/needn't* watering. It rained last night.

Task 3 Translate the following sentences into English.

1. 今年政府不敢再加税了。
2. 你应当更多地探望你的父母。
3. 隔壁那屋很嘈杂，他们准是在开晚会。
4. 他推荐了一两本他们可以买的书。
5. 天那样黑，我们什么也看不见。

Self-evaluation

Rate your own progress in this unit.	D	M	P	F*
I can say what is campus recruitment in English.	☐	☐	☐	☐
I can tell the ways of campus recruitment in English.	☐	☐	☐	☐
I can successfully be involved in campus recruitment.	☐	☐	☐	☐
I can build campus recruitment strategies.	☐	☐	☐	☐
I can write a letter of application.	☐	☐	☐	☐
I can master the usages of modal verbs.	☐	☐	☐	☐

*Note: D (Distinction), M (Merit), P (Pass), F (Fail)

Culture

在面试过程中，必不可少的程序就是面试官会先提出这个问题："请你先做个自我介绍吧。"高明的面试官会在你的自我介绍中考查你的逻辑思维和沟通表达能力。那么问题来了，一个满分的自我介绍到底要介绍哪些内容？

自我介绍和求职岗位核心能力要挂钩

好的自我介绍要围绕与该职位匹配的核心能力展开。

自我介绍的最终目的是向面试官简明扼要地说明你是他要找的人选，同时预埋伏笔引导你们接下来的谈话。真正的高匹配的答案，一定要凸显出你在任职方面的优势。

言简意赅，重点突出

一般情况下，2分钟的时间正常语速可以说300~350词，去掉前面的个人信息部分和必要的客套，你需要用300词把你的教育经历、职业经历和其他你认为重要的信息交代清楚。

总而言之，一个准备充分的应征者应该在面试前尝试用文字形式总结自己相关的工作经历和成就，重点介绍自身的强项和优势，并清晰阐述自己对未来的展望。在面试前反复练习，最终做到能够自然流畅地做好自我介绍。

 Task 1 Watch the following video clip, and then complete the mind map with missing words and phrases.

The formula for answering the question "Tell me about yourself"

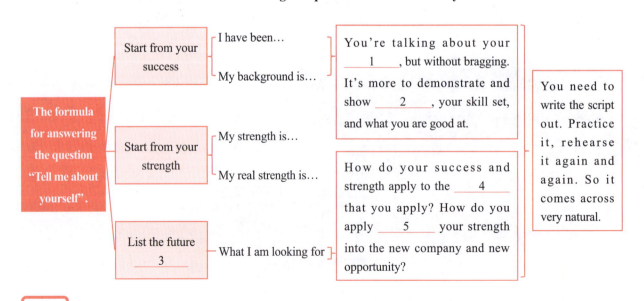

Task 2 Write a script for your answer to the question "Tell me about yourself."

New words & expressions

Unit 1

Reading A

New words

*tuition /tjuːˈɪʃn/	n. 学费		*critical /ˈkrɪtɪkl/	a. 批评的；批判的
▲imperative /ɪmˈperətɪv/	a. 必要的；势在必行的		*explore /ɪkˈsplɔː/	v. 探索；探究
prep /prep/	n. 预备，准备		*semester /sɪˈmestə/	n. 学期
*specific /spɪˈsɪfɪk/	a. 特定的；明确的		internship /ˈɪntɜːnʃɪp/	n. 实习；实习岗位；（学生或毕业生的）实习期
*relevant /ˈreləvənt/	a. 相关的；贴切的；中肯的		▲definitely /ˈdefɪnɪtli/	ad. 明确地；肯定地
▲discipline /ˈdɪsəplɪn/	n. 学科		*aspect /ˈæspekt/	n. 方面
syllabus /ˈsɪləbəs/	n. 教学大纲		▲foster /ˈfɒstə/	v. 促进；培养
*advanced /ədˈvɑːnst/	a. 先进的；高级的		*passion /ˈpæʃn/	n. 激情；热情
*seminar /ˈsemɪnɑː/	n. 讨论会；研讨班		undergrad /ˈʌndəɡræd/	n. 大学（本科）生
coursework /ˈkɔːswɜːk/	n. 课程作业		burgeoning /ˈbɜːdʒənɪŋ/	a. 迅速发展的；繁荣的
*loan /ləʊn/	n. 贷款			
*statistics /stəˈtɪstɪks/	n. 统计；统计学		requisite /ˈrekwɪzɪt/	a. 必备的，必不可少的
▲economics /ˌiːkəˈnɒmɪks/	n. 经济学			
*figure /ˈfɪɡə/	n. 数字			

Phrases & expressions

check out	核实；查实		keep in mind	牢记；放在心上
take out	取得，获得，领到（贷款、执照、保单等）		be likely to do something	可能做……
			engage with	忙于；从事

write off	注销；放弃	web developer	网站开发员
provide... with...	为……提供……	actuarial mathematics	精算数学；保险统计数学
have no idea	对……一无所知		
play the field	不专一；四处探索	graduate school	研究生院
make the most of	充分利用	liberal arts	文科；人文科学
vice versa	反之亦然	critical thinking	批判性思维
earn a degree	获得学位	general education course	通识课程
day trader	做短线者；当日交易者	introductory course	入门课程；基础课程
physical therapist	理疗师		

Reading B

New words

*mere /mɪə(r)/	a. 仅仅的	▲rewarding /rɪˈwɔːdɪŋ/	a. 值得做的；有益的
▲sustain /səˈsteɪn/	v. 使维持	▲therapist /ˈθerəpɪst/	n. 治疗专家
▲stable /ˈsteɪbl/	a. 稳定的	aeronautics /ˌeərəˈnɔːtɪks/	n. 航空学
*guarantee /ˌɡærənˈtiː/	n. 保证；担保	▲aviation /ˌeɪviˈeɪʃn/	n. 航空
*promising /ˈprɒmɪsɪŋ/	a. 有前途的；有希望的	▲pose /pəʊz/	v. 造成（威胁、问题等）；提问
▲compensation /ˌkɒmpenˈseɪʃn/	n. 薪酬；报酬；赔偿（金）	▲academics /ˌækəˈdemɪks/	n. 学习；学术
*facility /fəˈsɪləti/	n. 设施；设备	*airline /ˈeəlaɪn/	n. 航空公司
*annual /ˈænjuəl/	a. 每年的；一年一次的	pharmacology /ˌfɑːməˈkɒlədʒi/	n. 药物学；药理学
▲project /prəˈdʒekt/	v. 规划；估计		
*obtain /əbˈteɪn/	v. 获得；得到	pharmacist /ˈfɑːməsɪst/	n. 药剂师

Phrases & expressions

suit one's interests	适合某人的兴趣	power plant	发电厂
fondness for	喜爱……	unemployment rate	失业率
in demand	很受欢迎；需求量大	average salary	平均工资
when it comes to	一谈到……；当提到……时	college degree	大学学位
		employment rate	就业率
field of study	专业领域；研究领域	airplane manufacturer	飞机制造商

Unit 2

Reading A

New words

▲autonomous /ɔːˈtɒnəməs/	a.	自主的；自发的	*feedback /ˈfiːdbæk/	n. 反馈
▲innovation /ˌɪnəˈveɪʃn/	n.	创新，革新	*pursue /pəˈsjuː/	v. 从事；追求
▲innovative /ˈɪnəveɪtɪv/	a.	创新的	*objective /əbˈdʒektɪv/	n. 目标
*enormous /ɪˈnɔːməs/	a.	巨大的	*virtual /ˈvɜːtʃuəl/	a. 虚拟的
*possibility /ˌpɒsəˈbɪləti/	n.	可能性	*witness /ˈwɪtnəs/	v. 目击；见证
*present /prɪˈzent/	v.	展现；描述	artificially /ˌɑːtəˈfɪʃəli/	ad. 人工（造，为）地；不自然地
▲workout /ˈwɜːkaʊt/	n.	锻炼；健身	*intelligent /ɪnˈtelɪdʒənt/	a. 智能的；有智力的
*install /ɪnˈstɔːl/	v.	安装	*reaction /riˈækʃn/	n. 反应
*shift /ʃɪft/	v.	转移；变换	▲determine /dɪˈtɜːmɪn/	v. 决定
▲curriculum /kəˈrɪkjələm/	n.	课程	*manner /ˈmænə(r)/	n. 方式
*log /lɒg/	n.	日志	*derive /dɪˈraɪv/	v. 源于；获得
	v.	把……载入日志	▲augment /ɔːgˈment/	v. 增加；增大
*error /ˈerə(r)/	n.	误差；错误	*application /ˌæplɪˈkeɪʃn/	n. 应用程序
▲accommodate /əˈkɒmədeɪt/			*agenda /əˈdʒendə/	n. 议程；日程表
	v.	使适应		
*guidance /ˈgaɪdns/	n.	指导；引导		

Phrases & expressions

refer to	指的是	self-directed learner	自主学习者
work on	致力于，从事于	autonomous learning	自主学习
move through	完成；穿过	student-centered learning	以学生为中心的学习
derive at	得出	teaching curriculum	教学课程
innovative spirit	创新精神	autonomous classroom	自主学习课堂
self-driving car	自动驾驶汽车	self-monitoring strategy	自我监控策略
driverless car	无人驾驶车	error analysis	失误分析
future-ready thinkers	面向未来的思想家	chemical reaction	化学反应
self-driving student	自我驱动的学生	augmented reality	增强现实

Reading B

New words

personalize	/ˈpɜːsənəlaɪz/	vt. 使个性化	*rearrange	/ˌriːəˈreɪndʒ/	vt. 重新排列
*analyze	/ˈænəlaɪz/	vt. 对……进行分析	▲instructor	/ɪnˈstrʌktə(r)/	n. 教员；指导者
*current	/ˈkʌrənt/	a. 现在的	syllabi	/ˈsɪləbaɪ/	n. 摘要（syllabus 的复数）
*effective	/ɪˈfektɪv/	a. 有效的，起作用的	*calculate	/ˈkælkjuleɪt/	vi. 计算
▲productive	/prəˈdʌktɪv/	a. 富有成效的	*intensive	/ɪnˈtensɪv/	a. 加强的；集中的
*retain	/rɪˈteɪn/	vt. 保持；记住	*assignment	/əˈsaɪnmənt/	n. 作业；功课
*evaluate	/ɪˈvæljueɪt/	vt. 评价；估价	▲specifically	/spəˈsɪfɪkli/	ad. 特别地；明确地
▲digital	/ˈdɪdʒɪtl/	a. 数字的	*assess	/əˈses/	v. 对……进行评估
*calendar	/ˈkælɪndə(r)/	n. 日历；记事本	*accomplish	/əˈkʌmplɪʃ/	vt. 完成；实现
▲standing	/ˈstændɪŋ/	a. 长期存在的；永久性的；常设的	▲due	/djuː/	a. 到期的
▲commitment	/kəˈmɪtmənt/	n. 不得不做的事	*adjust	/əˈdʒʌst/	vt. 调整，使……适合
*available	/əˈveɪləbl/	a. 可获得的	▲consistently	/kənˈsɪstəntli/	ad. 一贯地
			*switch	/swɪtʃ/	v. 替换；转换

Phrases & expressions

base on	基于……；以……为根据	get the most out of	充分利用；发挥……的最大功效
get started on	开始做	stick to	坚持……
block out	挡住；遮挡	learning style	学习方式；学习风格
speak for	预定得到……；占用	study habits	学习习惯
leave little room for	几乎没有留下空间	blocks of time	整块时间
cut back on	削减；缩减	extracurricular activity	课外活动
set aside	留出	study session	学习时间（段）
add… to	增加；增添		

Unit 3

Reading A

New words

*imply	/ɪmˈplaɪ/	v. 意味；暗示	*contain	/kənˈteɪn/	v. 包含；含有

*essential /ɪˈsenʃl/	a. 基本的；必要的		placement /ˈpleɪsmənt/	n. 就业；(对人的)安置，安排
▲methodology /ˌmeθəˈdɒlədʒi/	n. 方法学，方法论		*prospect /ˈprɒspekt/	n. 可能性；希望；前景
*attach /əˈtætʃ/	v. 贴上；系上		*premise /ˈpremɪs/	n. 办公场所
▲theoretical /ˌθɪəˈretɪkl/	a. 理论的；理论上的		*motivate /ˈməʊtɪveɪt/	v. 激励；成为……的动机
*vital /ˈvaɪtl/	a. 至关重要的			
*flexible /ˈfleksəbl/	a. 灵活的；柔韧的		▲attentive /əˈtentɪv/	a. 留心的，注意的
*utilize /ˈjuːtəlaɪz/	v. 利用		*enhance /ɪnˈhɑːns/	v. 提高；加强
*authority /ɔːˈθɒrəti/	n. 当局；权威		outbound /ˈaʊtbaʊnd/	a. 出境的；向外去的
▲participation /pɑːˌtɪsɪˈpeɪʃn/	n. 参与		*subsidize /ˈsʌbsɪdaɪz/	v. 资助；给予奖助金
▲youngster /ˈjʌŋstə(r)/	n. 年轻人；少年		*beneficial /ˌbenɪˈfɪʃl/	a. 有益的，有利的
*outline /ˈaʊtlaɪn/	v. 概述；显示……的轮廓		facilitate /fəˈsɪlɪteɪt/	v. 促进；帮助
*appeal /əˈpiːl/	n. 吸引力，魅力		competitiveness /kəmˈpetətɪvnəs/	n. 竞争(力)

Phrases & expressions

attach importance to	重视		theoretical learning	理论学习
shape up	形成		on-the-job training	岗位培训；在职培训
apply... to...	把……应用于		administrative work	行政工作
work out	制定出		frontline service	一线服务
in line with	与……一致		placement training	就业培训
in view of	鉴于		team building	团队建设
on-campus training	校内实训		summer exchange program	暑期交换生项目
practical learning	实践学习			

Reading B

New words

*gap /gæp/	n. 缺口；间隔；差距		*financial /faɪˈnænʃl/	a. 金融的；财务的
▲academic /ˌækəˈdemɪk/	n. 学术知识		▲deliver /dɪˈlɪvə(r)/	vt. 交付；发表
*finance /ˈfaɪnæns/	n. 财政；金融		analyst /ˈænəlɪst/	n. 分析者
*former /ˈfɔːmə(r)/	a. 前者的；前任的		efficiency /ɪˈfɪʃnsi/	n. 效能；功效
valuation /ˌvæljuˈeɪʃn/	n. 评价，估价		▲display /dɪˈspleɪ/	vt. 展示；显露，表现
*live /laɪv/	a. 实况转播的，现场表演的		▲recruitment /rɪˈkruːtmənt/	n. 招收，招聘
			*expose /ɪkˈspəʊz/	vt. 使曝光，使暴露

▲core /kɔː(r)/	n. 核心；要点	▲comprehensive /ˌkɒmprɪˈhensɪv/	a. 详尽的；综合性的
▲associate /əˈsəʊsɪeɪt/	n. 同事；伙伴；合伙人 a. 有关联的	▲vulnerable /ˈvʌlnərəbl/	a. 易受攻击的，易受伤害的
uphill /ˌʌpˈhɪl/	a. 上坡的；向上的	▲articulate /ɑːˈtɪkjuleɪt/	vt. 明确表达；清楚说明
*version /ˈvɜːʃn/	n. 版本	follow-up /ˈfɒləʊ ʌp/	n. 后续行动；后续事物
▲exposure /ɪkˈspəʊzə(r)/	n. 暴露；曝光		a. 后继的；跟进的
overview /ˈəʊvəvjuː/	n. 概述；纵览；概论	▲concise /kənˈsaɪs/	a. 简明的；简洁
▲encounter /ɪnˈkaʊntə(r)/	v. 遭遇；邂逅		

Phrases & expressions

bridge the gap	缩小差距	Financial & Valuation Modeling Boot Camp 财务与估值建模新兵训练营	
pick up	拾起；捡起		
leave off	停止，中断	financial and valuation modeling skill set	财务与估值建模技能
succeed in (doing) something	在……上取得成功		
step by step	一步一步地；逐步地	financial industry	金融业
career center	就业中心	M&A (=merge and acquisition)	并购,兼并与收购
student club	学生俱乐部		
investment banker	投资银行家	leveraged buyout	融资收购；融资买入
		technical follow-ups	技术跟进

Unit 4

Reading A

New words

*community /kəˈmjuːnəti/	n. 社区；共同体	*significant /sɪɡˈnɪfɪkənt/	a. 有意义的
*benefit /ˈbenɪfɪt/	v. 有益于,对……有益 n. 利益,好处	*fortunate /ˈfɔːtʃənət/	a. 幸运的
		*advance /ədˈvɑːns/	v. 提升；促进；推进
*positive /ˈpɒzətɪv/	a. 积极的；肯定的	▲organizational /ˌɔːɡənaɪˈzeɪʃənl/	a. 组织方面的
*connect /kəˈnekt/	v. 连接,连结		
▲volunteer /ˌvɒlənˈtɪə(r)/	n. 志愿者 v. 自愿；做自愿者	*merely /ˈmɪəli/	ad. 仅仅
		*leap /liːp/	v. 跳跃；突然做

▲commitment /kə'mɪtmənt/	n. 承诺；（对工作或某活动）奉献，投入	*establish /ɪ'stæblɪʃ/	v. 建立，创立
		*perform /pə'fɔːm/	v. 执行；完成
		firsthand /'fɜːst'hænd/	a. 第一手的；直接的；亲身的
▲awareness /ə'weənəs/	n. 意识；认识	existing /ɪɡ'zɪstɪŋ/	a. 现存的；现有的
▲broaden /'brɔːdn/	v. 使扩大；使变宽	*strengthen /'streŋθn/	v. 加强；巩固
*horizon /hə'raɪzn/	n. 地平线；视野；眼界	introvert /'ɪntrəvɜːt/	n. 内向的人
		*socialize /'səʊʃəlaɪz/	v. 交际；参与社交
*issue /'ɪʃuː/	n. 问题	diverse /daɪ'vɜːs/	a. 不同的，多样的
*involve /ɪn'vɒlv/	v. 牵涉；包含；使陷于	surroundings /sə'raʊndɪŋz/	n. 环境；周围的事物
*individual /ˌɪndɪ'vɪdʒuəl/	n. 个人，个体		

🗩 Phrases & expressions

give back to	回馈；回报；归还	get involved	参与；介入
have effect on	对……有影响	have problems doing something	做……有困难
in need	贫困的；困难中的		
lie in	在于	community service	社区服务
try out	尝试，实验	organizational skill	组织能力
broaden one's horizons	开阔……的眼界	social awareness	社会意识

Reading B

📖 New words

▲donate /dəʊ'neɪt/	v. 捐赠，捐献		师；导师
impair /ɪm'peə/	v. 损害	counselor /'kaʊnsələ(r)/	n. 顾问；法律顾问
▲charity /'tʃærəti/	n. 慈善机构（或组织）；慈善；赈济；博爱	grocery /'ɡrəʊsəri/	n. 食品杂货店；食品杂货
		belongings /bɪ'lɒŋɪŋz/	n. 财产，所有物
▲auction /'ɔːkʃn/	n. 拍卖	homebound /'həʊmbaʊnd/	a. 回家的，回家乡的
▲makeup /'meɪkʌp/	n. 化妆品；组成	*sponsor /'spɒnsə(r)/	v. 赞助；发起；主办
▲perfume /'pɜːfjuːm/	n. 香水；香味	*update /ʌp'deɪt/	v. 更新
▲abuse /ə'bjuːz/	v. 虐待；滥用	carpool /'kɑːpuːl/	n. 合伙用车者；拼车
*tutor /'tjuːtə(r)/	v. 辅导；当指导教师 n. 家庭教师；指导教	reduce /rɪ'djuːs/	v. 减少；缩小
		▲emission /ɪ'mɪʃn/	n. 排放；排放物

*shelter /ˈʃeltə(r)/	n. 庇护；避难所	graffiti /ɡrəˈfiːti/	n. 涂鸦；墙上乱画（graffito 的复数形式）
perishable /ˈperɪʃəbl/	a.（食物等）易腐烂的；易变质的 n. 易腐品；非耐用品	*bare /beə(r)/	a. 空的；赤裸的，无遮蔽的
▲kit /kɪt/	n. 成套设备；全套衣服及装备	*campaign /kæmˈpeɪn/	n. 运动；活动
shampoo /ʃæmˈpuː/	n. 洗发水；香波	▲trash /træʃ/	n. 垃圾；废物
*sort /sɔːt/	v. 将……分类；整理	run-down /ˌrʌn ˈdaʊn/	a. 破败的；衰弱的
▲donation /dəʊˈneɪʃn/	n. 捐款，捐赠		
▲certify /ˈsɜːtɪfaɪ/	v. 证明；保证		

Phrases & expressions

clean up	清扫；清理，清除	soup kitchen	流动厨房；贫民救济处
Red Cross	红十字会	food bank	食物银行；食物储蓄站
community blood drive	社区献血活动		
charity race	慈善比赛	care kit	护理包
charity auction	慈善拍卖	homeless shelter	无家可归者收留所
retirement home	养老院；敬老院	first aid kit	急救包
senior center	老年中心；老年活动中心	certified lifeguard	注册救生员
		crossing guard	交通管理员
car emissions	汽车尾气	elementary school	小学

Unit 5

Reading A

New words

▲frequently /ˈfriːkwəntli/	ad. 频繁地；经常地；屡次	*estate /ɪˈsteɪt/	n. 大片私有土地；住宅区
*regular /ˈreɡjələ(r)/	a. 有规律的，定时的；经常的	*entry /ˈentri/	n. 进入；入口
*essentially /ɪˈsenʃəli/	ad. 本质上；基本上	*typically /ˈtɪpɪkli/	ad. 典型地；通常；一贯地
*credit /ˈkredɪt/	n. 学分 v. 获得学分	▲graduation /ˌɡrædʒuˈeɪʃn/	n. 毕业
▲corporate /ˈkɔːpərət/	a. 公司的；企业的	not-for-profit /ˌnɒt fə ˈprɒfɪt/	a. 非赢（营）利的

high-paying	/ˈhaɪ ˈpeɪɪŋ/	a.	高薪的	paycheck	/ˈpeɪtʃek/	n. 薪水
*competitive	/kəmˈpetətɪv/	a.	竞争的；好胜的；有竞争力的	sponsorship	/ˈspɒnsəʃɪp/	n. 赞助；支持
				chairperson	/ˈtʃeəpɜːsn/	n. 主席
▲likelihood	/ˈlaɪklihʊd/	n.	可能性，可能	*assume	/əˈsjuːm/	v. 假定，设想
*investment	/ɪnˈvestmənt/	n.	投资；投入	▲absolute	/ˈæbsəluːt/	a. 绝对的
intern	/ˈɪntɜːn/	n.	实习生	▲necessity	/nəˈsesəti/	n. 必然性；必需品
		v.	实习；做实习生	▲ultimately	/ˈʌltɪmətli/	ad. 最后；根本；基本上
vie	/vaɪ/	v.	激烈竞争；争夺			
groom	/gruːm/	v.	使做好准备；培养			

💬 Phrases & expressions

have nothing to do with	与……无关	job interview	求职面试
go out of one's way to do something	尽力做……	full-time job	全职工作
		people in charge	负责人
vie for	争夺……；竞争……	open position	空缺职位
be the case	是这样；是这种情况	university career services department	
real estate	房地产		大学就业服务中心
entry level position	初级职位	corporate internship	公司实习

Reading B

📖 New words

*strategy	/ˈstrætədʒi/	n.	战略，策略	parlay	/ˈpɑːleɪ/	v. 使增值；充分利用
*recommendation	/ˌrekəmenˈdeɪʃn/			*invest	/ɪnˈvest/	v. 投资；覆盖；耗费
		n.	推荐；建议；推荐信	activism	/ˈæktɪvɪzəm/	n. 行动主义；激进主义
*seek	/siːk/	v.	寻找；寻求；谋求	▲sample	/ˈsɑːmpl/	n. 样品，样本；（化验的）抽样
▲deadline	/ˈdedlaɪn/	n.	最终期限；截止期限			v. 品尝；体验
*additional	/əˈdɪʃnl/	a.	附加的，额外的	▲faculty	/ˈfæklti/	n. 全体教员
alumni	/əˈlʌmnaɪ/	n.	校友；毕业生（alumnus的复数）	*contact	/ˈkɑːntækt/	n. 联系；触摸 v. 联系，与……交往
*professional	/prəˈfeʃnl/	n.	专业人员；职业运动员	▲option	/ˈɒpʃn/	n. 选项；选择权；买卖的特权
▲prior	/ˈpraɪə(r)/	a.	先前的；优先的	▲expertise	/ˌekspɜːˈtiːz/	n. 专门知识；专门技术
*identify	/aɪˈdentɪfaɪ/	v.	确定；鉴定；识别			

subscribe	/səbˈskraɪb/	v. 订阅；认购	screen	/skriːn/	n. 屏幕；屏风 v. 筛选；审查
specialize	/ˈspeʃəlaɪz/	v. 专门从事；详细说明；特化	talented	/ˈtæləntɪd/	a. 有才能的；多才的
offline	/ˌɒfˈlaɪn/	a. 未联网的；脱机的	recruiter	/rɪˈkruːtə(r)/	n. 招聘人员；征兵人员
classify	/ˈklæsɪfaɪ/	v. 分类；分等	geographic	/ˌdʒɪəˈɡræfɪk/	a. 地理（上）的；地区（性）的

Phrases & expressions

stand a chance of doing…	有机会做……	lead time	提前期；前置时间
make connections with…	关联，联系	Career Services Office	就业服务中心
prior to	在……之前	career fields	职业领域
making a difference	有影响	college advisor	大学指导老师
subscribe to	定期订购（或订阅等）	career counselor	职业咨询师
specialize in	专门研究（从事）；专攻	career options	职业选择
		classified ads	分类广告
be of value	有积极作用，有意义	Career Fairs	招聘会

Unit 6　Reading A

New words

candidate	/ˈkændɪdeɪt/	n. 应试者，应聘者	designation	/ˌdezɪɡˈneɪʃn/	n. 委任；选派
merit	/ˈmerɪt/	n. 优点；价值；功绩	platform	/ˈplætfɔːm/	n. 平台；站台；月台
pipeline	/ˈpaɪplaɪn/	n. 管道；传递途径	ease	/iːz/	n. 自在；无忧无虑
target	/ˈtɑːɡɪt/	v. 瞄准；面向；对准	regarding	/rɪˈɡɑːdɪŋ/	prep. 关于；至于
institution	/ˌɪnstɪˈtjuːʃn/	n. （大学、银行等）机构	technologically	/ˌteknəˈlɒdʒɪkəli/	ad. 技术上地
foremost	/ˈfɔːməʊst/	a. 最重要的；最前的	incline	/ɪnˈklaɪn, ˈɪnklaɪn/	v. （使）倾向于；有……的趋势；（使）倾斜
possess	/pəˈzes/	v. 拥有，持有			
fulfill	/fʊlˈfɪl/	v. 履行；实现；满足	hence	/hens/	ad. 因此；由此
jot	/dʒɒt/	v. 匆忙记下；略记；摘要记载下来	allure	/əˈlʊə(r)/	v. 吸引；引诱
			spice	/spaɪs/	v. 在……中加香料；给……增添趣味
introspective	/ˌɪntrəˈspektɪv/	a. 内省的；反省的			

▲impressive /ɪmˈpresɪv/	a. 给人留下深刻印象的；令人赞叹的	▲overall /ˌəʊvərˈɔːl/	a. 全面的；综合的；总体的
▲monotonous /məˈnɒtənəs/	a. 单调的；乏味的	shortlist /ˈʃɔːtlɪst/	v. 把……列入入围名单
		scoring /ˈskɔːrɪŋ/	n. 得分
▲criteria /kraɪˈtɪəriə/	n. 标准（criterion的复数）	▲accordingly /əˈkɔːdɪŋli/	ad. 因此，于是；相应地
		*concentrate /ˈkɒnsntreɪt/	v. 专注；专心致志
*aware /əˈweə(r)/	a. 意识到的；明白的；有……意识的	▲peak /piːk/	n. 山峰；最高点；顶点

💬 Phrases & expressions

fulfill the needs of	满足……的需求	the first and the foremost thing	第一要务
jot down	匆匆记下		
meet the expectations of	满足……的期望	social media platforms	社交媒体平台
feel at ease	释然；心里踏实；舒气	digital channel	数字频道
be inclined to do something	倾向于做……	job description (JD)	工作职责说明
spice up	增加香料，增添趣味	do's and don'ts	应该做什么及不应该做什么
be aware of	知道；意识到		
in terms of	在……方面；依据……	salary package	薪资福利；薪酬
		educational institutions	教育机构
drop in	顺道拜访；突然拜访	peak time	峰值时间
campus recruitment	校园招聘		

Reading B

📖 New words

▲impact /ˈɪmpækt/	n. 巨大影响；撞击	▲consistent /kənˈsɪstənt/	a. 始终如一的，一致的；坚持的
*swing /swɪŋ/	n. 行程；秋千		
*bay /beɪ/	n. 海湾；湖湾	*presence /ˈprezns/	n. 出席；在场；（某物的）存在
*budget /ˈbʌdʒɪt/	n. 预算，预算费		
tier /tɪə(r)/	n. 层；等级	*brand /brænd/	n. 商标；（商品的）品牌
*talent /ˈtælənt/	n. 人才；有才能的人；天资	*ambassador /æmˈbæsədə(r)/	n. 大使
▲ongoing /ˈɒnɡəʊɪŋ/	a. 仍在进行的；不断前进的	*potentially /pəˈtenʃəli/	ad. 可能地；潜在地

*insight /ˈɪnsaɪt/	n. 洞察力；观点	upperclassmen /ˌʌpəˈklɑːsmen/	n. 美国高年级学生
*impression /ɪmˈpreʃn/	n. 印象，感想；印记，压痕	▲robust /rəʊˈbʌst/	a. 强健的；健康的
*long-lasting /ˌlɒŋ ˈlɑːstɪŋ/	a. 持久的；长期的	▲database /ˈdeɪtəbeɪs/	n. 数据库，资料库
▲impulse /ˈɪmpʌls/	n. 推动力；脉冲；冲击	*significantly /sɪɡˈnɪfɪkəntli/	ad. 显著地；相当数量地

💬 Phrases & expressions

in full swing	在热烈进行中；处于兴盛阶段	in the long run	长远，终究
a couple of something	几个人；几件事物	Campus Recruitment Strategy	校园招聘策略
keep… at bay	控制……	fall semester	秋季学期；秋季班
be likely to do something	可能的，预料的	top schools	顶尖大学
consist of	由……构成	career fair	招聘会
reach out	伸手去取	campus events	校园活动
have a long-lasting impact	对……产生持久的影响	brand ambassador program	品牌大使计划
down the line	在某一时刻；在某一环节		

Glossary

A

				Unit	Reading
absolute	/ˈæbsəluːt/	a.	绝对的	5	A
abuse	/əˈbjuːz/	v.	虐待；滥用	4	B
academic	/ˌækəˈdemɪk/	n.	学术知识	3	B
academics	/ˌækəˈdemɪks/	n.	学习；学术	1	B
accommodate	/əˈkɒmədeɪt/	v.	使适应	2	A
accomplish	/əˈkʌmplɪʃ/	vt.	完成；实现	2	B
accordingly	/əˈkɔːdɪŋli/	ad.	因此，于是；相应地	6	A
activism	/ˈæktɪvɪzəm/	n.	行动主义；激进主义	5	B
additional	/əˈdɪʃnl/	a.	附加的，额外的	5	B
adjust	/əˈdʒʌst/	vt.	调整，使……适合	2	B
advance	/ədˈvɑːns/	v.	提升；促进；推进	4	A
advanced	/ədˈvɑːnst/	a.	先进的；高级的	1	A
aeronautics	/ˌeərəˈnɔːtɪks/	n.	航空学	1	B
agenda	/əˈdʒendə/	n.	议程；日程表	2	A
airline	/ˈeəlaɪn/	n.	航空公司	1	B
allure	/əˈlʊə(r)/	v.	吸引；引诱	6	A
alumni	/əˈlʌmnaɪ/	n.	校友；毕业生（alumnus的复数）	5	B
ambassador	/æmˈbæsədə(r)/	n.	大使	6	B
analyst	/ˈænəlɪst/	n.	分析者	3	B
analyze	/ˈænəlaɪz/	vt.	对……进行分析	2	B
annual	/ˈænjuəl/	a.	每年的；一年一次的	1	B
appeal	/əˈpiːl/	n.	吸引力，魅力	3	A
application	/ˌæplɪˈkeɪʃn/	n.	应用程序	2	A
articulate	/ɑːˈtɪkjuleɪt/	vt.	明确表达；清楚说明	3	B
artificially	/ˌɑːtɪˈfɪʃəli/	ad.	人工（造，为）地；不自然地	2	A
aspect	/ˈæspekt/	n.	方面	1	A
assess	/əˈses/	v.	对……进行评估	2	B

assignment	/əˈsaɪnmənt/	n.	作业；功课	2	B
associate	/əˈsəʊsieɪt/	n.	同事；伙伴；合伙人	3	B
		a.	有关联的		
assume	/əˈsjuːm/	v.	假定，设想	5	A
attach	/əˈtætʃ/	v.	贴上；系上	3	A
attentive	/əˈtentɪv/	a.	留心的，注意的	3	A
auction	/ˈɔːkʃn/	n.	拍卖	4	B
augment	/ɔːɡˈment/	v.	增加；增大	2	A
authority	/ɔːˈθɒrəti/	n.	当局；权威	3	A
autonomous	/ɔːˈtɒnəməs/	a.	自主的；自发的	2	A
available	/əˈveɪləbl/	a.	可获得的	2	B
aviation	/ˌeɪviˈeɪʃn/	n.	航空	1	B
aware	/əˈweə(r)/	a.	意识到的；明白的；有……意识的	6	A
awareness	/əˈweənəs/	n.	意识；认识	4	A

B

bare	/beə(r)/	a.	空的；赤裸的，无遮蔽的	4	B
bay	/beɪ/	n.	海湾；湖湾	6	B
belongings	/bɪˈlɒŋɪŋz/	n.	财产，所有物	4	B
beneficial	/ˌbenɪˈfɪʃl/	a.	有益的，有利的	3	A
benefit	/ˈbenɪfɪt/	v.	有益于，对……有益	4	A
		n.	利益，好处		
boost	/buːst/	v.	使增长；提升	3	A
brand	/brænd/	n.	商标；(商品的)品牌	6	B
broaden	/ˈbrɔːdn/	v.	使扩大；使变宽	4	A
budget	/ˈbʌdʒɪt/	n.	预算，预算费	6	B
burgeoning	/ˈbɜːdʒənɪŋ/	a.	迅速发展的；繁荣的	1	A

C

calculate	/ˈkælkjuleɪt/	vi.	计算	2	B
calendar	/ˈkælɪndə(r)/	n.	日历；记事本	2	B
campaign	/kæmˈpeɪn/	n.	运动；活动	4	B
candidate	/ˈkændɪdeɪt/	n.	应试者，应聘者	6	A
carpool	/ˈkɑːpuːl/	n.	合伙用车者；拼车	4	B
certify	/ˈsɜːtɪfaɪ/	v.	证明；保证	4	B
chairperson	/ˈtʃeəpɜːsn/	n.	主席	5	A
charity	/ˈtʃærəti/	n.	慈善机构（或组织）；慈善；赈济；博爱	4	B
classify	/ˈklæsɪfaɪ/	v.	分类；分等	5	B

commitment	/kəˈmɪtmənt/	n.	不得不做的事	2	B
commitment	/kəˈmɪtmənt/	n.	承诺；(对工作或某活动)奉献，投入	4	A
community	/kəˈmjuːnəti/	n.	社区；共同体	4	A
compensation	/ˌkɒmpenˈseɪʃn/	n.	薪酬；报酬；赔偿(金)	1	B
competitive	/kəmˈpetətɪv/	a.	竞争的；好胜的；有竞争力的	5	A
competitiveness	/kəmˈpetətɪvnəs/	n.	竞争(力)	3	A
comprehensive	/ˌkɒmprɪˈhensɪv/	a.	详尽的；综合性的	3	B
concentrate	/ˈkɒnsntreɪt/	v.	专注；专心致志	6	A
concise	/kənˈsaɪs/	a.	简明的；简洁的	3	B
connect	/kəˈnekt/	v.	连接，连结	4	A
consistent	/kənˈsɪstənt/	a.	始终如一的，一致的；坚持的	6	B
consistently	/kənˈsɪstəntli/	ad.	一贯地	2	B
contact	/ˈkɒntækt/	n.	联系；触摸	5	B
		v.	联系，与……交往	5	B
contain	/kənˈteɪn/	v.	包含；含有	3	A
core	/kɔː(r)/	n.	核心；要点	3	B
corporate	/ˈkɔːpərət/	a.	公司的；企业的	5	A
counselor	/ˈkaʊnsələ(r)/	n.	顾问；法律顾问	4	B
coursework	/ˈkɔːswɜːk/	n.	课程作业	1	A
credit	/ˈkredɪt/	n.	学分	5	A
		v.	获得学分		
criteria	/kraɪˈtɪəriə/	n.	标准(criterion 的复数)	6	A
critical	/ˈkrɪtɪkl/	a.	批评的；批判的	1	A
current	/ˈkʌrənt/	a.	现在的	2	B
curriculum	/kəˈrɪkjələm/	n.	课程	2	A

D

database	/ˈdeɪtəbeɪs/	n.	数据库，资料库	6	B
deadline	/ˈdedlaɪn/	n.	最终期限；截止期限	5	B
definitely	/ˈdefɪnətli/	ad.	明确地，肯定地	1	A
deliver	/dɪˈlɪvə(r)/	vt.	交付；发表	3	B
derive	/dɪˈraɪv/	v.	源于；获得	2	A
designation	/ˌdezɪgˈneɪʃn/	n.	委任；选派	6	A
determine	/dɪˈtɜːmɪn/	v.	决定	2	A
digital	/ˈdɪdʒɪtl/	a.	数字的	2	B
discipline	/ˈdɪsəplɪn/	n.	学科	1	A
display	/dɪˈspleɪ/	vt.	展示；显露，表现	3	B
diverse	/daɪˈvɜːs/	a.	不同的，多样的	4	A
donate	/dəʊˈneɪt/	v.	捐赠，捐献	4	B

donation	/dəʊˈneɪʃn/	n.	捐款,捐赠	4	B
due	/djuː/	a.	到期的	2	B

E

ease	/iːz/	n.	自在;无忧无虑	6	A
economics	/ˌiːkəˈnɒmɪks/	n.	经济学	1	A
effective	/ɪˈfektɪv/	a.	有效的,起作用的	2	B
efficiency	/ɪˈfɪʃnsi/	n.	效能;功效	3	B
emission	/ɪˈmɪʃn/	n.	排放;排放物	4	B
encounter	/ɪnˈkaʊntə(r)/	v.	遭遇;邂逅	3	B
enhance	/ɪnˈhɑːns/	v.	提高;加强	3	A
enormous	/ɪˈnɔːməs/	a.	巨大的	2	A
entry	/ˈentri/	n.	进入;入口	5	A
error	/ˈerə(r)/	n.	误差;错误	2	A
essential	/ɪˈsenʃl/	a.	基本的;必要的	3	A
essentially	/kəˈnekt/	ad.	本质上;基本上	5	A
establish	/ɪˈstæblɪʃ/	v.	建立,创立	4	A
estate	/ɪˈsteɪt/	n.	大片私有土地;住宅区	5	A
evaluate	/ɪˈvæljueɪt/	vt.	评价;估价	2	B
existing	/ɪɡˈzɪstɪŋ/	a.	现存的;现有的	4	A
expertise	/ˌekspɜːˈtiːz/	n.	专门知识;专门技术	5	B
explore	/ɪkˈsplɔː/	v.	探索;探究	1	A
expose	/ɪkˈspəʊz/	vt.	使曝光,使暴露	3	A
exposure	/ɪkˈspəʊʒə(r)/	n.	暴露;曝光	3	B

F

facilitate	/fəˈsɪlɪteɪt/	v.	促进;帮助	3	A
facility	/fəˈsɪləti/	n.	设施;设备	1	B
faculty	/ˈfæklti/	n.	全体教员	5	B
feedback	/ˈfiːdbæk/	n.	反馈	2	A
figure	/ˈfɪɡə/	n.	数字	1	A
finance	/ˈfaɪnæns/	n.	财政;金融	3	B
financial	/faɪˈnænʃl/	a.	金融的;财务的	3	B
firsthand	/ˈfɜːstˈhænd/	a.	第一手的;直接的;亲身的	4	A
flexible	/ˈfleksəbl/	a.	灵活的;柔韧的	3	A
follow-up	/ˈfɒləʊ ʌp/	n.	后续行动;后续事物	3	B
		a.	后继的;跟进的		
foremost	/ˈfɔːməʊst/	a.	最重要的;最前的	6	A
former	/ˈfɔːmə(r)/	a.	前者的;前任的	3	B

fortunate	/ˈfɔːtʃənət/	a.	幸运的	4	A
foster	/ˈfɒstə/	v.	促进；培养	1	A
frequently	/ˈfriːkwəntli/	ad.	频繁地；经常地；屡次	5	A
fulfill	/fʊlˈfɪl/	v.	履行；实现；满足	6	A

G

gap	/gæp/	n.	缺口；间隔；差距	3	B
geographic	/ˌdʒɪəˈgræfɪk/	a.	地理（上）的；地区（性）的	5	B
graduation	/ˌgrædʒuˈeɪʃn/	n.	毕业	5	A
graffiti	/grəˈfiːti/	n.	涂鸦；墙上乱画（graffito的复数形式）	4	B
grocery	/ˈgrəʊsəri/	n.	食品杂货店；食品杂货	4	A
groom	/gruːm/	v.	使做好准备；培养	5	A
guarantee	/ˌgærənˈtiː/	n.	保证；担保	1	B
guidance	/ˈgaɪdns/	n.	指导；引导	2	A

H

hence	/hens/	ad.	因此；由此	6	A
high-paying	/ˌhaɪ ˈpeɪɪŋ/	a.	高薪的	5	A
homebound	/ˈhəʊmbaʊnd/	a.	回家的，回家乡的	4	B
horizon	/həˈraɪzn/	n.	地平线；视野；眼界	4	A

I

identify	/aɪˈdentɪfaɪ/	v.	确定；鉴定；识别	5	B
impact	/ˈɪmpækt/	n.	巨大影响；撞击	6	B
impair	/ɪmˈpeə/	v.	损害	4	B
imperative	/ɪmˈperətɪv/	a.	必要的；势在必行的	1	A
imply	/ɪmˈplaɪ/	v.	意味；暗示	3	A
impression	/ɪmˈpreʃn/	n.	印象，感想；印记，压痕	6	B
impressive	/ɪmˈpresɪv/	a.	给人留下深刻印象的；令人赞叹的	6	A
impulse	/ˈɪmpʌls/	n.	推动力；脉冲；冲击	6	B
incline	/ɪnˈklaɪn, ˈɪnklaɪn/	v.	（使）倾向于；有……的趋势；（使）倾斜	6	A
individual	/ˌɪndɪˈvɪdʒuəl/	n.	个人，个体	4	A
innovation	/ˌɪnəˈveɪʃn/	n.	创新，革新	2	A
innovative	/ˈɪnəveɪtɪv/	a.	创新的	2	A
insight	/ˈɪnsaɪt/	n.	洞察力；观点	6	B
install	/ɪnˈstɔːl/	v.	安装	2	A
institution	/ˌɪnstɪˈtjuːʃn/	n.	（大学、银行等）机构	6	A

instructor	/ɪnˈstrʌktə(r)/	n.	教员；指导者	2	B
intelligent	/ɪnˈtelɪdʒənt/	a.	智能的；有智力的	2	A
intensive	/ɪnˈtensɪv/	a.	加强的；集中的	2	B
intern	/ˈɪntɜːn/	n.	实习生	5	A
		v.	实习；做实习生		
internship	/ˈɪntɜːnʃɪp/	n.	（学生或毕业生的）实习期	1	A
introspective	/ˌɪntrəˈspektɪv/	a.	内省的；反省的	6	A
introvert	/ˈɪntrəvɜːt/	n.	内向的人	4	A
invest	/ɪnˈvest/	v.	投资；覆盖；耗费	5	B
investment	/ɪnˈvestmənt/	n.	投资；投入	5	A
involve	/ɪnˈvɒlv/	v.	牵涉；包含；使陷于	4	A
issue	/ˈɪʃuː/	n.	问题	4	A

J

jot	/dʒɒt/	v.	匆忙记下；略记；摘要记载下来	6	A

K

kit	/kɪt/	n.	成套设备；全套衣服及装备	4	B

L

leap	/liːp/	v.	跳跃；突然做	4	A
likelihood	/ˈlaɪklihʊd/	n.	可能性，可能	5	A
live	/laɪv/	a.	实况转播的，现场表演的	3	B
loan	/ləʊn/	n.	贷款	1	A
log	/lɒɡ/	n.	日志	2	A
		v.	把……载入日志		
long-lasting	/ˌlɒŋ ˈlɑːstɪŋ/	a.	持久的；长期的	6	B

M

makeup	/ˈmeɪkʌp/	n.	化妆品；组成	4	B
manner	/ˈmænə(r)/	n.	方式	2	A
mere	/mɪə(r)/	a.	仅仅的	1	B
merely	/ˈmɪəli/	ad.	仅仅	4	A
merit	/ˈmerɪt/	n.	优点；价值；功绩	6	A
methodology	/ˌmeθəˈdɒlədʒi/	n.	方法学，方法论	3	A
monotonous	/məˈnɒtənəs/	a.	单调的；乏味的	6	A
motivate	/ˈməʊtɪveɪt/	v.	激励；成为……的动机	3	A

N

necessity	/nəˈsesəti/	n.	必然性；必需品	5	A
not-for-profit	/ˌnɒt fə ˈprɒfɪt/	a.	非赢（营）利的	5	A

O

objective	/əbˈdʒektɪv/	n.	目标	2	A
obtain	/əbˈteɪn/	v.	获得；得到	1	B
offline	/ˌɒfˈlaɪn/	a.	未联网的；脱机的	5	B
ongoing	/ˈɒnɡəʊɪŋ/	a.	仍在进行的；不断前进的	6	B
option	/ˈɒpʃn/	n.	选项；选择权；买卖的特权	5	B
organizational	/ˌɔːɡənaɪˈzeɪʃənl/	a.	组织方面的	4	A
outbound	/ˈaʊtbaʊnd/	a.	出境的；向外去的	3	A
outline	/ˈaʊtlaɪn/	v.	概述；显示……的轮廓	3	A
overall	/ˌəʊvərˈɔːl/	a.	全面的；综合的；总体的	6	A
overview	/ˈəʊvəvjuː/	n.	概述；纵览；概论	3	B

P

parlay	/ˈpɑːleɪ/	v.	使增值；充分利用	5	B
participation	/pɑːˌtɪsɪˈpeɪʃn/	n.	参与	3	A
passion	/ˈpæʃn/	n.	激情；热情	1	A
paycheck	/ˈpeɪtʃek/	n.	薪水	5	A
peak	/piːk/	n.	山峰；最高点；顶点	6	A
perform	/pəˈfɔːm/	v.	执行；完成	4	A
perfume	/ˈpɜːfjuːm/	n.	香水；香味	4	B
perishable	/ˈperɪʃəbl/	a.	（食物等）易腐烂的；易变质的	4	B
		n.	易腐品；非耐用品		
personalize	/ˈpɜːsənəlaɪz/	vt.	使个性化	2	B
pharmacist	/ˈfɑːməsɪst/	n.	药剂师	1	B
pharmacology	/ˌfɑːməˈkɒlədʒi/	n.	药物学；药理学	1	B
pipeline	/ˈpaɪplaɪn/	n.	管道；传递途径	6	A
placement	/ˈpleɪsmənt/	n.	就业；（对人的）安置，安排	3	A
platform	/ˈplætfɔːm/	n.	平台；站台；月台	6	A
pose	/pəʊz/	v.	造成（威胁、问题等）；提问	1	A
positive	/ˈpɒzətɪv/	a.	积极的；肯定的	4	A
possess	/pəˈzes/	v.	拥有，持有	6	A
possibility	/ˌpɒsəˈbɪləti/	n.	可能性	2	A
potentially	/pəˈtenʃəli/	ad.	可能地；潜在地	6	B
premise	/ˈpremɪs/	n.	办公场所	3	A

prep	/prep/	n.	预备,准备	1	A
presence	/ˈprezns/	n.	出席;在场;(某物的)存在	6	B
present	/prɪˈzent/	v.	展现;描述	2	A
prior	/ˈpraɪə(r)/	a.	先前的;优先的	5	B
productive	/prəˈdʌktɪv/	a.	富有成效的	2	B
professional	/prəˈfeʃnl/	n.	专业人员;职业运动员	5	B
project	/prəˈdʒekt/	v.	规划;估计	1	B
promising	/ˈprɒmɪsɪŋ/	a.	有前途的;有希望的	1	B
prospect	/ˈprɒspekt/	n.	可能性;希望;前景	3	A
pursue	/pəˈsjuː/	v.	从事;追求	2	A

R

reaction	/riˈækʃn/	n.	反应	2	A
rearrange	/ˌriːəˈreɪndʒ/	vt.	重新排列	2	B
recommendation	/ˌrekəmenˈdeɪʃn/	n.	推荐;建议;推荐信	5	B
recruiter	/rɪˈkruːtə(r)/	n.	招聘人员,征兵人员	5	B
recruitment	/rɪˈkruːtmənt/	n.	招收,招聘	3	B
reduce	/rɪˈdjuːs/	v.	减少;缩小	4	A
regarding	/rɪˈɡɑːdɪŋ/	prep.	关于;至于	6	A
regular	/ˈreɡjələ(r)/	a.	有规律的,定时的;经常的	5	A
relevant	/ˈreləvənt/	a.	相关的;贴切的;中肯的	1	A
requisite	/ˈrekwɪzɪt/	a.	必备的,必不可少的	1	A
retain	/rɪˈteɪn/	vt.	保持;记住	2	B
rewarding	/rɪˈwɔːdɪŋ/	a.	值得做的;有益的	1	B
robust	/rəʊˈbʌst/	a.	强健的;健康的	6	B
run-down	/ˌrʌnˈdaʊn/	a.	破败的;衰弱的	4	B

S

sample	/ˈsɑːmpl/	n.	样品,样本;(化验的)抽样	5	B
		v.	品尝;体验		
scoring	/ˈskɔːrɪŋ/	n.	得分	6	A
screen	/skriːn/	n.	屏幕;屏风	5	B
		v.	筛选;审查	5	B
seek	/siːk/	v.	寻找;寻求;谋求	5	B
semester	/sɪˈmestə/	n.	学期	1	A
seminar	/ˈsemɪnɑː/	n.	讨论会;研讨班	1	A
shampoo	/ʃæmˈpuː/	n.	洗发水;香波	4	B
shelter	/ˈʃeltə(r)/	n.	庇护;避难所	4	B
shift	/ʃɪft/	v.	转移;变换	2	A

shortlist	/ˈʃɔːtlɪst/	v.	把……列入入围名单	6	A
significant	/sɪgˈnɪfɪkənt/	a.	有意义的	4	A
significantly	/sɪgˈnɪfɪkəntli/	ad.	显著地；相当数量地	6	B
socialize	/ˈsəʊʃəlaɪz/	v.	交际；参与社交	4	A
sort	/sɔːt/	v.	将……分类；整理	4	B
specialize	/ˈspeʃəlaɪz/	v.	专门从事；详细说明；特化	5	B
specific	/spɪˈsɪfɪk/	a.	特定的；明确的	1	A
specifically	/spəˈsɪfɪkli/	ad.	特别地；明确地	2	B
spice	/spaɪs/	v.	在……中加香料；给……增添趣味	6	A
sponsor	/ˈspɒnsə(r)/	v.	赞助；发起；主办	4	B
sponsorship	/ˈspɒnsəʃɪp/	n.	赞助；支持	5	A
stable	/ˈsteɪbl/	a.	稳定的	1	B
standing	/ˈstændɪŋ/	a.	长期存在的；永久性的；常设的	2	B
statistics	/stəˈtɪstɪks/	n.	统计，统计学	1	A
strategy	/ˈstrætədʒi/	n.	战略，策略	5	B
strengthen	/ˈstreŋθn/	v.	加强；巩固	4	A
subscribe	/səbˈskraɪb/	v.	订阅；认购	5	B
subsidize	/ˈsʌbsɪdaɪz/	v.	资助；给予奖助金	3	A
surroundings	/səˈraʊndɪŋz/	n.	环境；周围的事物	4	A
sustain	/səˈsteɪn/	v.	使维持	1	B
swing	/swɪŋ/	n.	行程；秋千	6	B
switch	/swɪtʃ/	v.	替换；转换	2	B
syllabi	/ˈsɪləbaɪ/	n.	摘要（syllabus的复数）	2	B
syllabus	/ˈsɪləbəs/	n.	教学大纲	1	A

T

talent	/ˈtælənt/	n.	人才；有才能的人；天资	6	B
talented	/ˈtæləntɪd/	a.	有才能的；多才的	5	B
target	/ˈtɑːgɪt/	v.	瞄准；面向；对准	6	A
technologically	/ˌteknəˈlɒdʒɪkli/	ad.	技术上地	6	A
theoretical	/ˌθɪəˈretɪkl/	a.	理论的；理论上的	3	A
therapist	/ˈθerəpɪst/	n.	治疗专家	1	B
tier	/tɪə(r)/	n.	层；等级	6	B
trash	/træʃ/	n.	垃圾；废物	4	B
tuition	/tjuˈɪʃn/	n.	学费	1	B
tutor	/ˈtjuːtə(r)/	v.	辅导；当指导教师	4	B
		n.	家庭教师；指导教师；导师		
typically	/ˈtɪpɪkli/	ad.	典型地；通常；一贯地	5	A

U

ultimately	/ˈʌltɪmətli/	ad.	最后；根本；基本上	5	A
undergrad	/ˈʌndəɡræd/	n.	大学（本科）生	1	A
update	/ˌʌpˈdeɪt/	v.	更新	4	B
uphill	/ˌʌpˈhɪl/	a.	上坡的；向上的	3	B
upperclassmen	/ˌʌpəˈklɑːsmen/	n.	美国高年级学生	6	B
utilize	/ˈjuːtəlaɪz/	v.	利用	3	A

V

valuation	/ˌvæljuˈeɪʃn/	n.	评价，估价	3	B
version	/ˈvɜːʃn/	n.	版本	3	B
vie	/vaɪ/	v.	激烈竞争；争夺	5	A
virtual	/ˈvɜːtʃuəl/	a.	虚拟的	2	A
vital	/ˈvaɪtl/	a.	至关重要的	3	A
volunteer	/ˌvɒlənˈtɪə(r)/	a.	志愿者	4	A
		v.	自愿；做志愿者		
vulnerable	/ˈvʌlnərəbl/	a.	易受攻击的，易受伤害的	3	B

W

witness	/ˈwɪtnəs/	v.	目击；见证	2	A
workout	/ˈwɜːkaʊt/	n.	锻炼；健身	2	A

Y

youngster	/ˈjʌŋstə(r)/	n.	年轻人；少年		

Phrases & expressions

A

		Unit	Reading
a couple of something	几个人；几件事物	6	B
actuarial mathematics	精算数学；保险统计数学	1	A
add... to	增加；增添	2	B
administrative work	行政工作	3	A
airplane manufacturer	飞机制造商	1	B
apply... to...	把……应用于	3	A

attach importance to	重视	3	A
augmented reality	增强现实	2	A
autonomous classroom	自主学习课堂	2	A
autonomous learning	自主学习	2	A
average salary	平均工资	1	B

B

base on	基于……；以……为根据	2	B
be aware of	知道；意识到	6	A
be inclined to do something	倾向于做……	6	A
be likely to do something	可能做……	1	A
be of value	有积极作用，有意义	5	B
be the case	是这样；是这种情况	5	A
block out	挡住；遮挡	2	B
blocks of time	一段时间	2	B
brand ambassador program	品牌大使计划	6	B
bridge the gap	缩小差距	3	B
broaden one's horizon	开阔……的眼界	4	A

C

campus events	校园活动	6	B
Campus Recruitment Strategy	校园招聘策略	6	B
campus recruitment	校园招聘	6	A
car emissions	汽车尾气	4	B
care kit	护理包	4	B
career center	就业中心	3	B
career counselor	职业咨询师	5	B
career fair	招聘会	6	B
Career Fairs	招聘会	5	B
career fields	职业领域	5	B
career options	职业选择	5	B
Career Services Office	就业服务中心	5	B
certified lifeguard	注册救生员	4	B
charity auction	慈善拍卖	4	B
charity race	慈善比赛	4	B
check out	核实；查实	1	A
chemical reaction	化学反应	2	A

classified ads	分类广告	5	B
clean up	清扫；清理，清除	4	B
college advisor	大学指导老师	5	B
college degree	大学学位	1	B
community blood drive	社区献血活动	4	B
community service	社区服务	4	A
consist of	由……构成	6	B
corporate internship	公司实习	5	A
critical thinking	批判性思维	1	A
crossing guard	交通管理员	4	B
cut back on	削减；缩减	2	B

D

day trader	做短线者；当日交易者	1	A
derive at	得出	2	A
digital channel	数字频道	6	A
do's and don'ts	应该做什么及不应该做什么	6	A
down the line	在某一时刻；在某一环节	6	B
driverless car	无人驾驶车	2	A
drop in	顺道拜访；突然拜访	6	A

E

earn a degree	获得学位	1	A
educational institutions	教育机构	6	A
elementary school	小学	4	B
employment rate	就业率	1	B
engage with	忙于；从事	1	A
entry level position	初级职位	5	A
error analysis	失误分析	2	A
extracurricular activities	课外活动	2	B

F

fall semester	秋季学期；秋季班	6	B
feel at ease	释然；心里踏实；舒气	6	A
field of study	专业领域；研究领域	1	B
Financial & Valuation Modeling Boot Camp	财务与估值建模新兵训练营	3	B
financial and valuation modeling skill set	财务与估值建模技能	3	B

financial industry	金融业	3	B
first aid kit	急救包	4	B
fondness for	喜爱……	1	B
food bank	食物银行；食物储蓄站	4	B
frontline service	一线服务	3	A
fulfill the needs of	满足……的需求	6	A
full-time job	全职工作	5	A
future-ready thinkers	面向未来的思想家	2	A

G

general education course	通识课程	1	A
get involved	参与；介入	4	A
get started on	开始做	2	B
get the most out of	充分利用；发挥……最大功效	2	B
give back to	回馈；回报；归还	4	A
go out of one's way to do something	尽力做……	5	A
graduate school	研究生院	1	A

H

have a long-lasting impact	对……产生持久的影响	6	B
have effect on	对……有影响	4	A
have no idea	对……一无所知	1	A
have nothing to do with	与……无关	5	A
have problems doing something	做……有困难	4	A
homeless shelter	无家可归者收留所	4	B

I

in demand	很受欢迎；需求量大	1	B
in full swing	在热烈进行中；处于兴盛阶段	6	B
in line with	与……一致	3	A
in need	贫困的；困难中的	4	A
in terms of	在……方面；依据……	6	A
in the long run	长远，终究	6	B
in view of	鉴于	3	A
innovative spirit	创新精神	2	A
introductory course	入门课程；基础课程	1	A
investment banker	投资银行家	3	B

J

job description (JD)	工作职责说明	6	A
job interview	求职面试	5	A
jot down	匆匆记下	6	A

K

keep in mind	牢记；放在心上	1	A
keep… at bay	控制……	6	B

L

lead time	提前期；前置时间	5	B
learning style	学习方式；学习风格	2	B
leave little room for	几乎没有留下空间	2	B
leave off	停止，中断	3	B
leveraged buyout	融资收购；融资买入	3	B
liberal arts	文科；人文科学	1	A
lie in	在于	4	A

M

M&A (=merge and acquisition)	并购，兼并与收购	3	B
make connections with…	关联，联系	5	B
make the most of	充分利用	1	A
making a difference	有影响	5	B
meet the expectations of	满足……的期望	6	A
move through	完成；穿过	2	A

O

on-campus training	校内实训	3	A
on-the-job training	岗位培训；在职培训	3	A
open position	空缺职位	5	A
organizational skill	组织能力	4	A

P

peak time	峰值时间	6	A
people in charge	负责人	5	A
physical therapist	理疗师	1	A
pick up	拾起；捡起	3	B
placement training	就业培训	3	A
play the field	不专一；四处探索	1	A
power plant	发电厂	1	B
practical learning	实践学习	3	B
prior to	在……之前	5	B
provide... with...	为……提供……	1	A

R

reach out	伸手去取	6	B
real estate	房地产	5	A
Red Cross	红十字会	4	B
refer to	指的是	2	A
retirement home	养老院；敬老院	4	B

S

salary package	薪资福利；薪酬	6	A
self-directed learner	自主学习者	2	A
self-driving car	自动驾驶汽车	2	A
self-driving student	自我驱动的学生	2	A
self-monitoring strategy	自我监控策略	2	A
senior center	老年中心；老年活动中心	4	B
set aside	留出	2	B
shape up	形成	3	A
social awareness	社会意识	4	A
social media platforms	社交媒体平台	6	A
soup kitchen	流动厨房；贫民救济处	4	B
speak for	预定得到……；占用	2	B
specialize in	专门研究（从事）；专攻	5	B
spice up	增加香料，增添趣味	6	A
stand a chance of doing...	有机会做……	5	B
step by step	一步一步地；逐步地	3	B

stick to	坚持……	2	B
student club	学生俱乐部	3	B
student-centered learning	以学生为中心的学习	2	A
study habits	学习习惯	2	B
study session	学习时间（段）	2	B
subscribe to	定期订购（或订阅等）	5	B
succeed in (doing) something	在……上取得成功	3	B
suit one's interests	适合某人的兴趣	1	B
summer exchange program	暑期交换生项目	3	A

T

take out	取得，获得，领到（贷款、执照、保单等）	1	A
teaching curriculum	教学课程	2	A
team building	团队建设	3	A
technical follow-ups	技术跟进	3	B
the first and the foremost thing	第一要务	6	A
theoretical learning	理论学习	3	A
top schools	顶尖大学	6	B
try out	尝试，实验	4	A

U

unemployment rate	失业率	1	B
university career services department	大学就业服务中心	5	A

V

vice versa	反之亦然	1	A
vie for	争夺……；竞争……	5	A

W

web developer	网站开发员	1	A
when it comes to	一谈到……；当提到……	1	B
work on	致力于，从事于	2	A
work out	制定出	3	A
write off	注销；放弃	1	A

Proper names

F

Facebook　　脸书；脸谱网（创立于2004年2月4日，总部位于美国加利福尼亚州门洛帕克）

P

PayScale.com　　PayScale薪酬网（美国统计薪资收入的权威网站，拥有世界上最大、最完善的雇员薪酬数据库）

Y

YouTube　　"油管"视频网站（一家专供用户免费上传、观赏、分享视频的共享网站，创立于2005年2月15日，后被谷歌公司收购）